Is the
BIBLE
Necessary?

Al Provost

ISBN 978-1-63885-885-0 (Paperback)
ISBN 978-1-63885-886-7 (Digital)

Copyright © 2022 Al Provost
All rights reserved
First Edition

Scripture taken from the New King James Version®. Copyright © 1982 by Thomas Nelson. Used by permission. All rights reserved.

All rights reserved. No part of this publication may be reproduced, distributed, or transmitted in any form or by any means, including photocopying, recording, or other electronic or mechanical methods without the prior written permission of the publisher. For permission requests, solicit the publisher via the address below.

Covenant Books
11661 Hwy 707
Murrells Inlet, SC 29576
www.covenantbooks.com

Contents

Acknowledgments 5

Chapter 1: From Los Angeles to Madrid and Jerusalem 7
Chapter 2: First Ambassadors' Meeting 13
Chapter 3: Jury Selection 23
Chapter 4: Media 31
Chapter 5: Mr. Cobra's Opening Statement 35
Chapter 6: Mr. Devas's Opening Statement 39
Chapter 7: Dr. Garden: Fear and Death 49
Chapter 8: Dr. North: Errors in the Bible 54
Chapter 9: Dr. Powers: Opinions about the Bible 60
Chapter 10: Dr. Winter: The Humanist View 66
Chapter 11: Dr. Eagle: Character Flaws 75
Chapter 12: Dr. Lios: Archaeology 81
Chapter 13: Dr. Rubin: Bible Translations 91
Chapter 14: The Journalist Perspective 98
Chapter 15: Dr. Sandberg: The Bible Is Perfection 100
Chapter 16: Dr. Rubin (Continued) 109
Chapter 17: Dr. Lamb: Apologetics 112
Chapter 18: Prime Minister Jean Bernard: The Bible Helps 121
Chapter 19: Dr. Mary Graves: Why Jesus 129
Chapter 20: Mr. Cobra's Closing Statement 143
Chapter 21: Mr. Devas's Closing Statement 146
Chapter 22: The Jury Deliberates 154
Chapter 23: The Jury's Decision 157

ACKNOWLEDGMENTS

I dedicate this book to Jesus, who literally turned my life around and taught me to love and care about people and all of His creation. I also dedicate this work to Diane, my lovely wife of thirty-seven years, who helped edit and contributed to some of the writing.

Also, a special thanks to our friends Leslie Donahue and Terry Leach for their contributions. An additional thanks to the many pastors and professors who have discipled me over the years. Their varied college- and seminary-level classes greatly increased my knowledge and in-depth understanding of God's Word, the Bible.

CHAPTER 1

FROM LOS ANGELES TO MADRID AND JERUSALEM

Oh, how we had been waiting for this day! The kids were grown and on their own, and we had not had a vacation in years. We had been planning one in coordination with a business trip for over a year now. It was delayed initially for over six months because of a terrible worldwide pandemic. There were just no flights out of the United States to Europe, but now our excitement was building, as the day of departure was imminent.

Let me introduce myself. My name is Fred Jacobs, and I am a freelance journalist. My wife, Diane, has a degree in archaeology. Our home is on the Central Coast of California. We intended to use our education and experience in both these areas on our journeys overseas in the upcoming trip. Diane hoped to get involved with some digs when we got to some sites.

I'm one of those guys who have about a dozen journalist credentials; these allow me access to most functions around the world. I have studied many of the cultures in Europe and in surrounding countries. My degree in journalism and experience as a freelance journalist have enabled me to travel the world, writing stories about different cultures, religions, governments, etc. I do not work for any particular paper, magazine, or company, but I do submit the majority of my work to Mr. Ford at the magazine *Truth*, which he distributes to various organizations. Mr. Ford, who is a Christian and a man of integrity, will only accept articles that have been verified to be true.

Our flight was to leave LA at 5:00 p.m. on Monday. Well, the day arrived, and things got exciting right from the start. We had planned on stopping at a gas station before getting on the freeway. However, we started talking and drove right past the gas station and onto the freeway. We looked at each other in horror and started to pray, knowing that the next gas station was more than five miles away.

The car ran out of gas just before the off-ramp! Now with no power steering, our troubles increased. We prayed more as I guided the car onto the off-ramp, turned right onto the street, and right up next to a gas pump. The Lord saved us from being late for our flight. We thanked Jesus right on the spot.

We took a deep breath and are on our way. We boarded a plane in Los Angeles right on time, bound for New York, where we would catch a plane on Wednesday morning for Madrid, Spain. The takeoff from the Los Angeles airport was smooth, and clear skies provided a view for about one hundred miles and a beautiful sunset, thanks to the Lord. The plane made a U-turn and started our flight to New York.

As darkness set in and the view of the ground receded, we did some reading to prepare for our meetings in Madrid, Spain. It was a long flight to New York, so we did enjoy a little TV before arriving at 10:00 p.m., Monday (1:00 a.m., New York time). Upon arrival, we were not surprised that the airline had misplaced our luggage, but we trusted that the Lord would provide for our needs. A shuttle picked us up and drove us to our hotel, where we stayed two nights, giving us a casual day in New York.

Wednesday morning in New York was cold, windy, and misty. After breakfast, the shuttle drove us to the airport in time for our flight to Madrid. No luggage yet! Our plane left New York at 6:00 a.m., as the pilot stated that we might have rough weather flying over the Atlantic Ocean (the pond).

I had called the pastor of the Madrid Calvary Chapel, Pastor Rey, a few times before we left the United States, to set up a meeting. He had mentioned that the Universal Senate of World Religions (USWR) was a very negative organization toward Christianity and the Bible. There were some disturbing rumors about them in Europe. I had also called Professor Garcia, a religious studies professor at the University of Rosen, to set up a meeting.

We arrived in Madrid seven and a half hours after takeoff from New York. WOW! We were exhausted after a 3,600-mile nonstop flight. Still no luggage! The shuttle drove us to the door of our hotel, where we had time to relax, have a leisurely dinner, and then head straight to bed. Awakening the next morning somewhat refreshed but famished, we enjoyed breakfast at the hotel restaurant, which was a welcome treat after airplane food. Good news followed! Our luggage was found and delivered to the hotel. Thank You, Lord. Not sure if we were going to stay another night or two, we decided against unpacking our suitcases. Thankfully, the clerks at the front desk assured us that our room would be available if we decided to stay longer.

On the business side of our trip, I planned to investigate and write about various religions from different countries and how they interact with one another. I had spoken with Professor Garcia prior to leaving the United States and planned to meet with him while in Madrid. Although he was a religious studies professor, we believed that he was a true Bible-believing Christian.

When I called the professor, he asked us to come to his office that morning at 10:00. A taxi delivered us to his office, where we experienced a warm reception and a successful meeting. We were eager for him to share what he knew about a group called the Universal Senate of World Religions (USWR). The members were VERY ANTI-BIBLE, not believing that the Bible was needed anywhere. The professor did not have anything good to say about the USWR. However, we were not disappointed with the other useful information he provided for us.

After meeting with Professor Garcia, we decided to eliminate a portion of our tour of Madrid because we were concerned about the USWR. But we did hire a guide to show us around Madrid that afternoon. The driver took us through some beautiful residential areas, impressive commercial developments, and gorgeous parks and other sites. It was a treat having a tour guide as well as a chauffeur, even though I really enjoy driving in new cities. Diane and I hadn't been on a vacation for some time, so we really enjoyed visiting the tourist sites there in Madrid. Because our jobs kept us so very busy, we had very little time to enjoy each other's company, which made this trip very special. I must say that we did set aside a couple of days or evenings a month to spend exclusively with each other. Our children had been taught the importance of this practice since they were little.

After our tour, we called Pastor Rey, an acquaintance of ours who had visited us in the States. We made an appointment to meet him the next day for lunch and talk. We met his family and joined them for a very pleasant lunch at his lovely home in the countryside. Pastor Rey had previously mentioned that the **Universal Senate of World Religions (USWR)** was very negative toward Christianity and the Bible, and Professor Garcia had emphasized the same thing. Right at the start, we were shocked by what Pastor Rey had to say. First of all, he told us he believed this terrifying group (USWR) and others were conspiring to spread rumors that discredited the Bible. They were being backed by rich individuals and corporations worldwide.

After our talk with Pastor Rey, as per his suggestion, we called Jon Martin, the pastor at the Calvary Chapel Church in Lagoa, Portugal. We rented a car and traveled the next morning, Saturday, to Lagoa to speak with him for more information on the USWR. According to Pastor Rey, Pastor Jon was the most knowledgeable person concerning these rumors. None of us were sure what this was all about, but we were concerned that this organization, the USWR, was likely the group that had organized an effort to prevent the Bible from being printed. My wife and I intended to find the source of the USWR and the extent of this rumor and to investigate. I knew she would be a great asset with her writing and interviewing skills.

IS THE BIBLE NECESSARY?

View along the southern shores of Portugal

After making an appointment with Pastor Jon, we drove to Lagoa to meet with him. As we drove, we enjoyed refreshing sea breezes and beautiful landscapes, making for very pleasant conditions along the way although it was a warm day. It was a long drive, five hundred miles and seven hours at the 75 mph speed limit across southern Spain and into Portugal. This was a very important meeting, so we took turns driving to ensure that we would not be too tired by the time we reached our destination. Diane and I finally arrived in Lagoa, Portugal, where Pastor Jon had made reservations for us at a cozy hotel.

We rested before locating him at Calvary Chapel Church (Lagoa Christian Fellowship) for our meeting. Pastor Jon, who was also an attorney, informed us that the Universal Senate of World Religions was the main organization behind a lawsuit to eliminate the printing of the Bible. Over the last two thousand years, many individuals and organizations had tried to remove part or all of the Bible from all humanity. This may have been the largest effort yet!

This lawsuit had been filed quickly within the last few months by the powerful Universal Senate of World Religions. To make matters worse, most of the Christian churches and organizations knew nothing or very little about the lawsuit. So from that point, Pastor Jon and I, along with our wives, began spending all our time researching for any information we could find about this lawsuit. Just the thought of this lawsuit against the Bible was outrageous every way you looked at it.

We contacted Pastor Rey in Madrid to let him know that we were returning, and we set a meeting to update him on our findings. He indicated that he would invite other pastor friends to join us. Pastor Jon and his wife had visited many countries and cities to speak to pastors and their congregations about the necessity for all peoples and nations to read and study the Bible.

CHAPTER 2

FIRST AMBASSADORS' MEETING

Pastor Jon and I, along with our wives, drove to Madrid to meet with Pastor Rey. We acknowledged that we had to take the bull by the horns and put together a committee of Bible experts in Madrid to oppose this lawsuit, which would not allow any Bible to be printed anywhere in the world. Pastor Rey and Pastor Jon invited two of their pastor friends and their wives to join us, and we called our children, Mary and Joe, and asked them to fly to Madrid to join us. I also invited two of our close Bible-believing Christian friends to meet us in Madrid. They said that they would be very pleased to join us.

The first item on our agenda was to develop prayer teams to provide a constant spiritual covering for all our efforts. Without the Holy Spirit's guidance and wisdom, our work would prove to be futile.

The first committee would be made up of Pastor Rey, Pastor Jon, me, and our wives, along with a total of six friends and a total of eighteen adult children. This group of thirty people, comprising pastors, family, and personal friends, possessed a wide variety of university degrees and would call themselves the Ambassadors. Many additional people (pastors and others) for other committees would need to be approved by the Ambassadors. Some of the original thirty-six Ambassadors had already been sent to meet with pastors and Christian leaders in surrounding cities in Europe. As our numbers grew, we would be able to send more members "to the ends of the world." The Ambassadors prepared an agenda and would send the same agenda with all the committees so that all cities, countries, etc. that they would visit would have the same emphasis on the subject. We were blessed to have professional Bible translators to assist us by translating our agenda and anything else we needed into different languages.

We had to believe that the power of the Holy Spirit was with us and would continue to be with us and lead us to where He wanted us to go. And we had to emphasize that time was of the essence and that ongoing prayer was vital. We had just discovered that the United Atheists had secretly joined the Universal Senate of World Religions, who had already begun their attack on the Bible with TV ads and social media. Furthermore, we had to investigate which individuals and corporations were backing the USWR.

We rented a very spacious office building in downtown Madrid. Besides the offices, we purchased or rented computers, tablets, telephones, etc. There was enough room for twenty legal teams to work. We did not know where the trial would take place. There was much to do to prepare for this project, including hiring computer experts, Bible experts, and others, along with purchasing important equipment. The computers had to be loaded with all the relevant information and staffed by computer experts as soon as possible. But it may still take weeks to formulate. All the areas were under special security with lock and key, and there were guards outside and inside.

Once we selected our legal team, we would set up critical mock trials. This would help all involved with picking a jury and, most importantly, assist the lead attorney and his or her assistants. As necessary, the committees would meet with government officials in targeted cities to discuss important matters with the powers that be. We would listen to political speeches and spiritual sermons, go to seminars at churches and synagogues and temples, etc. The details of who, what, where, when, why, and how this lawsuit was proceeding had to be determined. We would speak to individuals, companies, organizations, etc. in order to prepare and answer questions.

While investigating and gathering information for trial preparation, we discovered that the responses from some of the people we visited were quite similar, whether from a government or a newspaper/magazine (media) official. They somehow knew we were Christian and refused to discuss anything about the lawsuit with us. Someone had obviously spread the word about our effort to defeat the lawsuit.

In an effort to acquire testimonies from representatives of most people groups and religious sects, in order to strengthen our investigations and studies, we had even reached out to atheist and agnostic groups to find a common ground and address their concerns. It was so important to influence worldwide opinion of the Bible before the trial. We were praying that all people, even those who differed from our beliefs, would understand the seriousness of the situation and that many would join us in our effort to defend the integrity of the Bible.

As qualified people were recruited and assigned to work as the "disciples of Jesus," committees would be formed to GO into all the world. Some volunteers would need to be trained in various cultures, as approved by the Ambassadors.

Within ten days of sending out thousands of letters, hundreds of responses from all around the world had been received, and most of the people whose names had been submitted were being vetted. Some countries were large in size or population, so we had to rely on the pastoral leaders of those countries to set up a network to reach as many churches as possible. How many committees (representatives) we would need and where they would go was yet to be determined. We had to consider the language, knowledge of scriptures, and the culture of the people we would visit, and assign each committee accordingly. Then we would send representatives to the European nations.

To start, there would be twelve representatives for these various countries. The African countries would also have twelve representatives. In South America, the countries would have a total of ten representatives. That's a total of thirty-four representatives needed in seventeen countries, along with two each for the United States, Russia, Philippines, Brazil, Mexico, and Nigeria, for a minimum total of forty-six representatives for twenty-three countries where most of the world's Christian population lived. All the representatives had to organize whatever number of groups in the countries they would serve. WOW!

We had thirty initial Ambassadors, but some of those had to stay at our home office. The Ambassadors had to recruit additional volunteers, who in turn would recruit individuals or groups of volunteers so that workers were available in all continents and in most countries. What a challenge!

The Ambassadors had to choose Bible-believing Christians for the first twenty-three countries that we had contacted and all countries thereafter. Time was of the essence.

As you can imagine, the finances for a project like this was unknown yet. What we did know was, it would take a tremendous amount of money. But thank the Lord, we had been richly blessed with a blank check by an anonymous donor. We all knew that this gift was strictly from God. We had put together a cash flow and a time flow chart in order to estimate the cost and time required for the trial. We had been notified that the trial would be in Jerusalem, but we didn't know the starting date.

So after three months of being in Madrid, we were able to find office space and housing in Jerusalem; we also rented vans (some folks loaned us their van; thank You, Jesus) and office equipment. The windows of the building could be opened, and one lady from our team noticed some doves landing on a couple of ledges. She placed some dove food on the ledges, and soon we had some beautiful solid-white doves come and visit every day. We loved to hear them coo. It was spiritual symbolism to us. The work to contact churches, individuals, and corporations to assist us would be very time-consuming.

We want to emphasize again that the result of what we were doing and accomplishing would be a difference of LIFE AND DEATH (physically, emotionally, and spiritually) for the whole world. The Universal Senate of World Religions had been meeting with Judge El-Bib, who would oversee the trial, and they were pushing for the trial to start within a few weeks. This forced the Ambassadors to request a later start time, which Judge El-Bib had allowed so far.

There are around 195 countries in the world. This required a concerted effort to inform as much of the world's population as possible through major news organizations and social media on all aspects of this very important trial.

There was more urgency for Christians to win this trial than all the other trials against Christianity, in total, throughout the history of mankind, except the trial against Jesus. You may ask, why the urgency? The answer is simple. If the verdict was not in favor of the Bible, not one Christian publisher or printer would be able to provide a Bible to anyone. Similar threats had been made throughout history, but this one was particularly ominous and funded by some powerful and wealthy individuals and organizations. We had to be very vigilant.

What was the principal weapon in our Christian arsenal against this threat? What must we do? The millions and even billions of Christians around the world had to repent and pray fervently to God the Holy Spirit for guidance, which would lead to knowledge and then understanding, and prayerfully give wisdom to our defense team. Also, **2 Chronicles 7:14 (NKJV)** says, "If My people who are called by My name will humble themselves, and pray and seek My face, and turn from their wicked ways, then I will hear from heaven, and will forgive their sin and heal their land." Enough said!

It had been about four weeks since the first thirty-four committees traveled to the thirty-four countries in Europe, South America, Africa, the USA, etc. Since then, these thirty-four committees had increased their number to over seventy to GO around the world. The Ambassadors would decide in the next few days which countries the new committees would visit. This would require each of the committee members (representatives) to travel thousands of miles in the next few days and weeks.

According to Open Doors USA, these are the most dangerous countries for Christians: North Korea, Afghanistan, Somalia, Sudan, Pakistan, Libya, Iraq, Yemen, Iran, India, Congo, and Saudi Arabia. Needless to say, should any of our committees venture into any of these countries, they had to be very vigilant in their approach to anyone. Of 7.7 billion people, only 2.4 billion people are Christians, which would be about a two-to-one ratio. Jesus told us in His Word that there are some things we cannot do on our own. It was going to take the strength and the power of the Holy Spirit to overcome this power of **the Universal Senate of World Religions**, which was outwardly backed by Satan. There was evidence throughout the Bible that Satan was trying to kill Jesus; he knew who Jesus was. With that in mind, the Ambassadors' subgroups went to work.

Concentrating on the job at hand, the Ambassadors had to continue to contact people around the world who were concerned about religious freedom and Christians whose main concern was saving the Bible. Additional work included hiring lawyers who were experts in international law, secretaries, and biblical scholars. We were rushed for time but blessed financially. Praise the Lord! A few of our volunteers would work on raising additional finances as the need arose for transportation, lodging, office space, and equipment.

Hiring a lead attorney was of primary importance for the Ambassadors. We knew many attorneys but NEEDED the one the LORD wanted. There were thousands of good lawyers in the world; we needed the best. Hundreds of letters had been sent out requesting resumes. The interview committee, which included lawyers selected from the original Ambassadors, would interview each acceptable applicant as soon as possible. Before each interview, the interview committee would pray that the Holy Spirit would provide guidance to choose the one and only person in the world who should be our lead lawyer.

Working almost around the clock, the interview committee managed to interview eighty-seven lawyers from around the world in four weeks, evaluating each one by ten standards previously set up to grade the applicants. Whew, what a whirlwind of activity. In a four-week period, the field had been reduced to eight people—four women and four men who had made the cut, you might say. It appeared that any one of them would have made a perfect lead lawyer. These applicants were advised that the lead lawyer would need assistance, and three of the applicants agreed to take that position if not selected as the lead lawyer.

The interview committee then decided to set aside two days for prayer and review all their notes on the candidates. Selecting the lead attorney for this trial was undoubtedly the most important aspect of this whole case so far. Within the last hour, the committee completed interviewing all applicants.

There was no one in our building except our committee and the security guards. Remember, we said that our offices were securely locked, with security guards inside and outside, on the streets and on the roof. Suddenly, we heard heavy footsteps coming down the hallway and right past the security guard. We were all very startled to see a man in his early thirties boldly walk into our office. He was dressed impeccably, with neatly trimmed raven-colored hair and a beard. He wore a knee-length coat over dress slacks, with sandals on his feet. The coat consisted of four very rich colors: red, white, purple, and gold. He displayed a commanding presence as he walked confidently in our direction, not in a menacing way but as one who was cool and unflappable.

When asked who he was, why he was here, and of course, how he got into our offices and past the guards, he did not answer but simply looked around the room at each one of us and asked his own question: "Why are you here?" We were shocked by his boldness and were unsure how to answer this stranger. Silence ensued for what seemed an eternity. Looking around the room, everyone was quiet, as if this man standing in front of us had us all tongue-tied.

Finally, the silence was broken as someone asked him again why he was here. Was he interested in joining our legal team, and did he have the qualifications? When he simply nodded, we asked him again, "How are you qualified?"

He answered, "If you are truly Bible scholars, as you say you are, you would know who I am." With that startling statement, he stood up, looked around the room at each of us, bowed his head, and walked out.

A few of us followed after this mystery man, but he was gone in no time! We asked the guards where he went, but they said that they saw no one come from our office. Fascinated by this remarkable individual, we all agreed that somehow we must find him and interview him, although it seemed he had been interviewing us.

*****

Judge El-Bib, the presiding judge over this lawsuit, was using court case *MacLennan v. Morgan Sindall* (December 30, 2013; EWHC 4044[QB]) for civil evidence as the main research/source document for rule changes. On January 7, 2014, the defendant in the *MacLennan v. Morgan Sindall* case applied under rule 32.2(3), which gave the judge express powers to identify and/or limit the number of witnesses an attorney may call. That power was now being used by this judge.

Judge El-Bib was born in Moscow in 1955, migrated to Israel in 1969, and has served on the bench for twenty-five years and on the Universal Court since 2002. He contacted Mr. Cobra and Pastor Jon Martin to meet in his office the next morning at 8:00. Pastor Jon Martin was the Ambassador's spokesman until an attorney was hired.

The judge wanted to discuss the trial, especially the time element for its completion. He believed that people around the world would get very impatient if the trial took too long. He feared there was a possibility the trial could take up to a year, and he considered that totally unacceptable. Therefore, he made a decision that both sides would be allowed no more than six witnesses and that each witness would be restricted to covering two subjects only.

*****

After two full days of reviewing the resumes of the eight remaining applicants, the twelve Ambassadors were again confronted by the stranger who called himself Joshua, who had simply appeared in our office. We asked him again why he was here. Looking at us with piercing eyes, he answered, "What do you want from me?" We responded that there was a need for a competent, qualified lawyer on our legal team. We asked him if he had the experience required. His answer was astounding! He said without hesitation, "The fact is, I wrote the laws." Then he wanted to know what we needed to defend. We disclosed to him that the Universal Senate of World Religions was putting the Bible on trial in an attempt to eliminate it and to make it illegal to print a Bible.

IS THE BIBLE NECESSARY?

At that point, Joshua told us that his full name was Joshua Devas and that he would serve as the lead attorney to defend the Bible.

We were startled that this stranger was so bold, claiming to be the lead attorney when we had not interviewed him or offered the position to him. Mr. Devas was then told that the Ambassadors would discuss the matter and get back to him. When asked for his address and phone number, he simply answered that he would get back to us when the time was right. Of course, we had no idea how he would know when the time was right. However, Mr. Devas had such an overpowering presence that we closed by stating that we would see him soon. A moment after he left the room, a cool but forceful wind passed through. With no fan in the room and no windows to the outside, we just stood there dumbfounded, looking at each other and wondering what had just happened.

As soon as Mr. Devas left the Ambassadors, we settled down from these very baffling events, a discussion of Mr. Devas's mysterious comments began. What did he mean when he said "The fact is, I wrote the laws"? Taken by surprise, we had been hesitant to ask him at the time. He had a dignified air about him that left us speechless. You can only imagine what areas our conversation covered after he left.

The next day, Sunday, we all attended church together and were able to relax for a few hours with our families. But we were preoccupied, knowing how essential it was to stay on top of our main objective, which was to hire a lead attorney. So on Monday, we met again to review and discuss the eight applications that had come to us, and of course, to talk about Mr. Devas. The twelve Ambassadors deliberated on all eight applicants for about the next five hours. All applicants had excellent references. Three applicants had master's degrees and five had doctorate degrees, mainly in theology. Then the discussion came around to Mr. Devas, who had given us no resume, application, degrees in education, or job references. We needed to know what law firms he had worked for and what cases he had prosecuted or defended.

After two more days, a few more meetings, and lots of prayer—and I mean lots of prayer—the Ambassadors, with help from the

Holy Spirit, made a decision to hire Mr. Devas. This decision was made on FAITH alone. We could claim no other answer. Our vote was unanimous.

Finishing up some paperwork and questioning whether we were doing the right thing by hiring Mr. Devas, we remembered that there was no way to get in touch with him. However, on Thursday morning, this problem faded away within ten minutes of our arrival at the committee meeting room when, all of a sudden, Mr. Devas appeared in our office as if he knew we needed to see him. When told that he was hired to be the lead attorney, he simply nodded with composure and sat down.

We mentioned to Mr. Devas that three of the eight qualified people who would like to assist him in the proceedings were Miss Wright, Mrs. Christian, and Mr. Law. Mr. Devas stated that these particular choices would be excellent additions to his legal team, especially because of their lifelong dedication to preserving the Bible's integrity. (How would he know that? We had never shared any applicant's resume with him.) He then revealed to us that he had selected SH to be his second chair. We had no idea who this SH person was or what the initials stood for. And SH was not one of the original applicants, so obviously he/she had not been interviewed. We couldn't figure out Mr. Devas's strategy or his tremendous ability to persuade us, but we submitted to his will by the power of the Holy Spirit.

As the Ambassadors brainstormed for trial preparation, a very important topic came to light. We needed expert jury and witness selection criteria, which included people with knowledge of body language and developing appropriate questions. So a special subcommittee was formed to handle this venture.

The question came up early about whether there would be a grand jury or preliminary hearing, but Judge El-Bib emphatically said, "NO!" The judge also clarified that this trial would be a civil trial and not a criminal trial.

Effort for prayer: We were sure the media wouldn't favor our side, so all Christians were encouraged to be gracious in words and actions, as rallies must be peaceful, bathed in prayer, and a godly witness of love and grace for the world.

CHAPTER 3

JURY SELECTION

All the Ambassadors believed that everyone should use the Bible in all aspects of their lives. They also believed that the Bible was inerrant, that it was perfect. No one should be allowed to remove or add to any portion of the Bible. I repeat that no portion of the Bible should be changed. Jesus Christ Himself said in **Matthew 24:35 (NKJV)**, "Heaven and earth will pass away, but My words will by no means pass away."

The next step was for the Ambassadors to start preparing for the mock trial in an effort to anticipate any argument that might be used to destroy the Bible. There was a lot of work ahead and not much time, so everyone was anxious to get started. Twelve of the Ambassadors formed a large committee to research questions for prospective jurors for the mock trial. The questions asked of actual trial jurors would be the same or similar to the ones used for the mock jury. The actual jury would most likely be a cross section of nationalities, religions, and cultures, prompting the Ambassadors to select twenty-five people as representative samples to serve on the mock jury. The Ambassadors (twelve of them) would also research questions to ask our witnesses.

The Ambassadors wasted no time in remodeling one of the larger rooms in our office space. It now resembled the courtroom where the actual trial would be conducted in the city of Jerusalem in Israel.

To select the official jury of the Bible's "peers," there was a lot of brainstorming required. That was why the mock jury and mock trial were very important. Just who or what were the Bible's peers? We had to and would win this trial for the benefit of the whole world.

The selection of the mock jury and the procedure of the mock trial lasted three and a half days, but it went extremely well. The Ambassadors, Joshua Devas, and his staff were satisfied and believed that we were ready. Three Ambassadors were assigned to study different cultures within the four major religions: Islam, Buddhism, Hinduism, and Christianity, which make up the majority of people on all seven continents. The study required, therefore, would be daunting.

Culture means "(1) the customary beliefs, social forms, and material traits of racial, religious, or social groups; (2) the characteristic features of everyday existence shared by people in a certain place." For example, the Middle East consists of approximately twenty countries, with many different religions (but mainly Islamic) and a variety of ethnic and linguistic groups. They share sets of traditions, belief systems, and behaviors shaped by culture, history, religion, ethnic identity, language, and nationality, among other factors. The information gathered by our committee would help us formulate questions to be used during jury selection to determine individual cultural beliefs. The relevancy of culture would be disclosed during the trial proceedings.

Four of our Ambassadors, Pastor Jon Martin, Miss Wright, Mrs. Christian, and Mr. Law, would be on a committee to investigate and recruit two more scholars of the Bible to be expert witnesses. They would also research questions to ask prospective witnesses and brainstorm the possible subjects that Mr. Cobra may use to prosecute the Bible. Four expert witnesses, Dr. Rubin, Dr. Graves, Dr. Sandberg, and Dr. Lios had already been selected.

Two Ambassadors would be needed for additional aspects of our case. The mock jury trial and the actual trial would be in Jerusalem, in the country of Israel. These two Ambassadors would travel to Jerusalem and set up our office space that we rented three months ago.

Three of the Ambassadors who applied for the lead attorney position, Miss Wright, Mrs. Christian, and Mr. Law, were psychologists as well as lawyers and had volunteered to assist in the case. They would be extremely helpful in analyzing the words and actions of the prospective jurors. There is a saying that actions speak louder than words, and that is so very true. By going through a mock trial, we would observe the jurors as we ask them questions and analyze their answers and reactions.

We may ask the jurors if they had ever read the Bible or other religious books, like the Koran, the Hadith, the Vedas, or the Tripitaka. The Koran and the Hadith are the books of the Muslim faith, written about AD 600. The Vedas, or Books of Knowledge, are the foremost sacred texts in Hinduism, which were written between 1500 BC and 1000 BC. The Tripitaka, the sacred Buddhist writings, were actually named after the language spoken by the Buddha and were composed between 550 BC and 1 BC.

A juror's answer about the Bible may be "Sure, I read the Bible every year," or it may be "Not at all." So just by observing the reactions of the jurors, we would have a pretty good indication how each juror felt about reading the Bible and how much they did it. On the other hand, the juror may answer, "What book are you talking about?" Many of the jurors may be familiar with the Koran, the Hadith, the Vedas, or the Tripitaka. Therefore, by studying these books, the Ambassadors would be somewhat knowledgeable about the cultures and the writings of other religions and groups.

After each witness in the mock trial, each juror would present a critique concerning the questions and answers for each witness.

The actual jury selection process begins

The first step of the jury selection was the request by the trial court judge for the first thirty potential jurors, selected randomly from around the world, to be directed to a private room. The prospective jurors would be given an IQ test in English only. Although not legal in many countries, the judge and the attorneys felt it was important, even though the jurors would not be told the nature of the test. This short test would be graded quickly before the jurors would be dismissed. We were accepting only jurors with IQs over

110. The prospective jurors with a test score under 110 would be dismissed and sent home.

The next step in the process would take place in the courtroom, where the prospective jurors would be required to swear truthfully and answer all questions asked of them about their qualifications to potentially serve as jurors in this particular case. This swearing is called the perjury admonishment (an authoritative statement made to the jury by the judge regarding their conduct as jurors).

Afterward, the jurors would be questioned by both the judge and the prosecuting and defense attorneys. The purpose of questioning was to determine any biases or prejudices the juror may have that could affect the juror's judgment. Both attorneys and the judge were looking for jurors who would be as impartial as possible. This process is called voir dire, an old French phrase meaning "a preliminary examination of a witness or a juror by a judge and/or counsel."

The prospective jurors were encouraged to ask for clarifications when questions by the attorneys were not understood. The psychologists on the defense team would be extremely helpful in using sign language to relay comments to the lead attorney. The judge would then explain to the jurors their legal obligations while serving on the jury, and request that any juror who believed he/she could not follow the regulations should ask to be excused for cause. The jurors would be told that they were going to be sequestered for as much as a month or two. There would be no regular TV, newspapers, magazines, or personal electronic devices in their hotel rooms. After being sworn in, the jurors would be given a questionnaire, to be completed within an hour. After the questionnaires were collected and a copy given to the judge and all attorneys, the judge would request that the jury report to the jury room until the judge and attorneys finished reviewing the questionnaires.

Questionnaire (Detail your answers!)

Can there ever be world peace? _____
Do you believe in GOD or a god? _____
Do you believe Satan is real? _____

IS THE BIBLE NECESSARY?

Did you graduate high school? _____
Did you graduate college? _____
Where do you currently work? _____
Are you a supervisor? _____
Are you a member of any organizations? _____
Have you ever served on a jury? _____
Do you believe in evolution? _____
Does everyone have a spirit? _____
Does everyone have a soul? _____
Do you read books? _____
Can reading the Bible help people? _____
Do you believe in eternal life? _____
Do you believe in heaven and hell? _____
Do you believe in good and evil? _____
Have you sued someone or been sued? _____
Do you smoke, drink, or use drugs? _____

Judge El-Bib asked the bailiff to bring the jurors into the courtroom. He then read the perjury admonishment clause to the prospective jurors: "I understand and agree that I will accurately and truthfully answer, under penalty of perjury, all questions propounded to me concerning my qualifications and competency to serve as a trial juror in the matter pending before this court, and that failure to do so may subject me to criminal prosecution." He then asked, "Do you understand and accept this responsibility?" All answered, "I do."

The Ambassadors (the psychologists) in the gallery also received a copy of the completed questionnaires, enabling them to assist in the jury selection by using sign language to relay comments and questions to Mr. Devas. The judge called on Mr. Devas to ask his first question for the jury.

"Ladies and gentlemen of the jury, please raise your hand if you believe that you have an answer to this question. What do you believe is needed for world peace?"

Juror number two raised his hand and answered, "We should all have the same language."

Juror number seven said, "We should all have a more similar culture."

Mr. Cobra then approached the jury and asked, "What about military force?"

Juror number four countered, "If we want to have peace, why should there be a military?"

Mr. Cobra replied, "History tells us that without military, it's impossible to have peace."

It took a week for the whole jury selection process, but it was worth it. In all, thirteen groups of jurors came through. Four jurors were accepted in the first group of jurors, one in the second, and so on, until twelve jurors and four alternates were accepted. The judge and attorneys agreed that these jurors qualified to decide impartially and intellectually on the factual issues in the case. Judge El-Bib declared that this jury was official.

There could be no communication with the outside world during the trial. Therefore, Judge El-Bib instructed the jurors that all their electronic devices would be collected by the bailiff. He asked the jurors to place labels on their phones, watches, and any other electronic devices, and the bailiff would collect them separately. This was done since there could be no communication with the outside world during the trial, as a standard precautionary procedure. All of the jury's electronic valuables would be kept in separate safes located in the judge's office. The valuables would be guarded twenty-four hours a day by two UN guards on each shift during the entire trial. All the jurors were given the phone number of the courtroom, which was to be given to their contact person, only to be used in an emergency. Each juror would be given a tablet, and they were told that they may take notes. The notes may be used during deliberations.

The bailiff then approached the jury and asked them to listen carefully as the judge read the general oath for jurors. This oath was different than the perjury admonishment. Judge El-Bib asked the jury to stand, raise their right hand, and repeat after him. "'I swear that I will fairly try the case before this court and that I will return a true and honest verdict according to the evidence and the instruc-

IS THE BIBLE NECESSARY?

tions of this court under the punishment of the law.' If you understand this oath, say 'I do.'" All the jurors answered, "I do."

The names of the final jurors must only be shared with the judge, the two attorneys, and the bailiff.

BELOW IS INFORMATION ABOUT THE JURORS.

Truck driver	Female	White	45
Retail store manager	Male	Hispanic	65
Court clerk	Male	Black	28
Artist	Female	Black	38
Carpet layer	Male	Asian	27
Engineer (electrical)	Female	Asian	44
Dentist	Female	Middle Eastern	60
Nurse	Male	White	31
Lawyer	Male	Indian	41
Chef	Female	Hispanic	58
Housewife	Female	Jewish	33
Writer	Male	White	53

The alternates were a janitor, a doctor, a CEO, and a fireman.

Judge El-Bib pounded his gavel and announced that the trial would begin tomorrow morning at 10:00. The bailiff directed the gallery to be cleared and informed the jury that each day of deliberation they would receive the lunch of their choice from the hotel menu. This lunch would be eaten in the jury room at the large table in the back of the room. Breakfast and dinner, however, would be served in the hotel dining room. After all the jury instructions were complete, the jurors returned to their hotel rooms with the UN guards.

Each of the jurors would have a private hotel room on the same floor, where two guards would be stationed when their rooms were occupied. Only the streaming of movies and TV shows would be available, but no live TV shows. The jurors may bring in personal books and papers from home or work, subject to the approval of the judge. All the rooms would have a computer but would not have access to the Internet. The computer would be loaded with many works from various religions, along with a large Bible search program, a concordance, commentaries, and a Greek/Hebrew lexicon. In addition, the computers would have a copy of the Koran, the Hadith, the Vedas, the Tripitaka, the Book of Mormon, and other writings that Mr. Cobra may request. These would be available during the length of the trial.

YOU, THE READER OF THIS BOOK, ARE THE THIRTEENTH JUROR. WHEN YOU HAVE COMPLETED READING THIS BOOK, YOU WILL HAVE A VOTE. SO CONSIDER ALL THE EVIDENCE AND COMMENTS CAREFULLY. WHICH SIDE HAS THE TRUTH?

Chapter 4

Media

It was Friday, 8:00 a.m. The trial was due to begin at 10:00 a.m., and I, Fred Jacobs, was in the courtroom to observe the proceedings. Some of the Ambassadors (leaders for the defense team) were also waiting in the gallery, as were some other observers with permits to attend this first day of the trial. The courtroom gallery was filled with people.

I moved outside to the front of the courthouse. This very first day of the trial found the weather to be an ominous prelude to a daunting task, with heavy dark-gray clouds surrounding the entire city of Jerusalem. The clouds gave the appearance that the rains would spill out of them at any moment. It was almost as if the clouds were holding the trial participants and observers hostage.

Despite this cold, windy weather, there were people with chairs, umbrellas, and blankets covering the sidewalks, courtyards, and grass areas as far as a half mile from the courthouse. I walked in the midst of this crowd about a block from the courthouse, observing the actions and reactions of the crowds. Surprisingly, camping around the courthouse had been allowed by special permit and only in specified locations. The camping groups had conflicting views of the Bible but had been very peaceful. The police departments from Israel and Palestine, as well as peacekeepers from the UN, were posted all around the area of the courthouse to ensure peace. TV screens had been set up around the area for all to see the testimonies.

The decision to broadcast the trial had been in itself a major issue. Only after Judge El-Bib was convinced that Israel, Palestine, and the UN would cooperate to ensure peace did he agree to allow the trial to be broadcast to the crowds on the street. The audio would come from one radio station, KNEW.

As the trial was about to begin, the whole world was in a spiritual uproar, reaching fever pitch. In the weeks and months leading up to the start of the trial, there had been a tremendous increase of violence throughout the world, especially against Christians. To some people, just the idea that the Bible was on trial had to mean that the Bible was wrong and shouldn't be printed by anyone. But certain world religions feared that their holy books may be subjected to the same scrutiny, so some had become Christianity's unlikely allies. The Universal Senate of World Religions was the main organization that had hired Mr. Cobra to prosecute the Bible. Atheist associations and other fringe groups had become their allies.

This trial would be under the auspices of the Universal Court (UC), which was established in 2002 and was an intergovernmental organization and international tribunal that sat in Petah Tikva. However, this trial had been moved to Jerusalem, in Israel.

District Courthouse UC (Jerusalem)

IS THE BIBLE NECESSARY?

The UC jurisdiction covered the prosecution of individuals or entities for the international crimes of genocide, crimes against humanity, war crimes, and the crime of aggression.

It had been mentioned that this would be the trial of the millennium (it would be like two young rams butting heads). There had been trials about evolution, about the separation of church and state, and about religious free speech in the public square. But not since the trial of Jesus Christ two thousand years ago had there been a trial that questioned an individual's fundamental belief system, the foundation of one's very life! Today that trial began. The Bible was on trial for its life. Would it survive? If it did not, it would be illegal to print the Bible anywhere in the world. The verdict in this case had worldwide ramifications, and it was not known how each side would react upon the decision of the jury. This created tremendous pressure on the jury. To stop printing the Bible would be disastrous for Christianity. History tells us that no free society has survived very long without the Bible.

I talked to a man on the street in the Cobra camp. "Sir, what do you think will take place if the Bible is found guilty?"

"There is no doubt in my mind that the UN and local police will check publishers for any new printing and demand that it stop."

Here was a lady who was in the Devas camp. I asked, "What do you think will happen if the Bible is found to be guilty?"

"I'm not sure what will take place, but what I do know is that the Lord Jesus told us and really commanded us to spread His Word throughout the world."

I then returned to the steps of the courthouse to speak with some friends. Bill, Sarah, and Diego were discussing that the easy flow of the Bible made it appear to have been written by one person. Bill said there was a verse in the Bible that said it was inspired by God so that we may be able to do good works. A lady standing nearby said the Bible was just a bunch of made-up stories and fables. With that, I left my friends and headed back into the courtroom.

Mr. Cobra and Mr. Devas were in the courtroom. Mr. Cobra was dressed in a very sharp charcoal gray suit with a light-burgundy shirt and a dark tie. His hair was short, and he was clean-shaven. Mr.

Devas was wearing a knee-length coat that had four different vertical colors and black slacks. His hair was neatly combed down to his collar, and he had a very short beard.

The sparkling clean courtroom was quite elaborate in appearance. The walls, doors, and even the desks were made of very rich-colored mahogany wood. The ceilings were twelve feet high with room dimensions of 60 × 40 feet. The judge's bench was four feet above everyone in the courtroom. The windows on each side of the room were open, unfortunately, because the air-conditioning and fans were not working. The temperature outside was 75° F and was expected to increase, but there was no way to move the trial to another court.

Judge El-Bib was about to come into the courtroom to begin the trial. One could feel both the excitement and tension coming from the people in the gallery and outside.

CHAPTER 5

MR. COBRA'S OPENING STATEMENT

It was 10:00 a.m. The bailiff called the jury into the courtroom from the jury room and asked all to stand as Judge El-Bib came into the courtroom. He motioned for everyone to be seated. Then the judge made the following announcement to the attorneys, the jury, and the people in the gallery: "Concerning the conduct of this court, if there are uproars, disturbances, or problems of any kind, I may be forced to clear the gallery and/or charge someone with contempt of court. To the jury, your verdict must be unanimous. And to the attorneys, any additional witnesses, exhibits, or physical evidence must be submitted to and approved by the court at least two days prior to introducing such items to the court. This trial is very important because it concerns the Bible of the Christians. The jury's decision will determine whether the printing of the Bible will be allowed in the future or not."

Judge El-Bib stated that the jury had been sworn in, and he asked both lawyers if they were ready to proceed. Mr. Cobra and Mr. Devas stated that they were. Judge El-Bib asked Mr. Cobra to begin his opening statement.

Mr. Cobra thanked the judge, rose from his chair, and walked to the area about seven feet in front of the jury. "Your Honor, ladies and gentlemen of the jury. My name is Mr. Cobra. I am an attorney, and I will be providing you with evidence that the defendant—" He paused. "—the Bible, is guilty, as it has been charged with the crimes of conspiracy, manipulation, trickery, connivance, and cover-up."

Mr. Cobra told the jury how important this trial was for the whole world. "We have been under the deception of this one book for way too long. Many, many people have been hurt emotionally, financially, and spiritually by the strict way the Bible demands that people run their lives.

"Today I come to you with a heavy heart. Christians have tried to promote information or technology in every field of science that has never helped society. And without exception, they have led mankind away from the freedom and liberty to individually decide one's own morality, and they have caused Christendom to stumble for centuries into an abyss of error and sorrow in a downward spiral.

"In view of the Bible's numerous mistakes about the physical and scientific world, there's no reason to believe that its writers were any more correct about unseen and abstract matters like heaven and hell. Being so greatly in error regarding the tangible and observable universe, the Bible cannot be considered a reliable guide for spiritual and ethical issues. My witnesses will elaborate further on various topics. They will present proof, if you will, about many different subjects that the Bible declares to be true but that are, in fact, false.

"We will present political and spiritual leaders who will testify that the Bible has caused people to riot, damage property, hurt people, and even kill. The Bible says in Matthew 26:51 (NKJV), 'And suddenly, one of those who were with Jesus [Peter] stretched out his hand and drew his sword, struck the servant of the high priest, and cut off his ear.'

"Christians say that the Bible is true and without error. But if we act as some verses in the Bible direct us, it will cause tremendous emotional and spiritual damage. Christians around the world are pushing this information on all people groups. How is it that they believe statements like 'Children will rise up against parents and cause them to be put to death'? That, in my mind, is a terrible, terrible image.

IS THE BIBLE NECESSARY?

"The failed prophecies in the Bible further strengthen the humanist view, which is a doctrine centered on human interests and values, especially a philosophy that rejects supernaturalism—" He paused shortly. "—and stresses an individual's dignity, worth, and capacity for self-realization through reason. One of our witnesses is a humanist. Because many Christian (biblical) prophecies turned out to be false, they prove the Bible is not true.

"Genesis 2:17 is one verse of many where the Bible is wrong. It states that the Lord warned Adam and Eve about the fruit on the tree of knowledge of good and evil, saying, 'In the day that thou eat thereof thou shalt surely die.' According to Genesis chapter 3, however, Adam and Eve ate the forbidden fruit and didn't die on that day, showing that the Bible is not without errors.

"Noah's Ark is a well-known story in the Bible. The story claims that God got angry with all the people on earth and decided that He would eliminate mankind and start over. So He talked with Noah and told him to build a big boat. Noah, his wife, his three sons, and their wives built the ark." Mr. Cobra paused. "Really? Just eight people built that big boat? Sometime later, God told Noah and his family to get into the ark. God also placed two of every kind of animal in the boat. It started to rain, and the rains eventually killed all people and animals that weren't in the ark. Now I say to you, ladies and gentlemen of the jury, is that a good God, and should the Bible tell stories like this? I say no, and therefore, it should not be printed ever again."

Mr. Cobra continued his dialogue for about five minutes, the whole time describing the failings of the Bible. And then he paused.

"We are told that humans have free will. If we have this so-called free will, why are we not allowed to leave an abusive spouse by divorce? If a woman is raped and gets pregnant, why not allow her to have an abortion to rid herself of the reminder of the horrific act?"

Looking at Mr. Devas, Mr. Cobra said, "In your Bible, one of the ten commandments states, 'Do not covet.' In other words, do not desire what belongs to another. Let's say your neighbor wears really fine clothes and drives an expensive car. What's wrong, really, with wanting what your neighbor has?"

Walking closer to the jury, he said, "I believe that you are all too smart to accept that the Bible is from some god. You know that it is full of errors, contradictions, and unbelievable stories. We will show that the Bible is no more than a crutch needed by people too weak to stand on their own. You will easily come to the conclusion that the Bible is guilty as charged and must not be printed anywhere in the world."

Mr. Cobra thanked the jury and the judge, turned to his chair, and sat down. Judge El-Bib thanked Mr. Cobra and stated that the court would reconvene after lunch, at 2:00 p.m.

CHAPTER 6

Mr. Devas's Opening Statement

It was 2:00 p.m., and the judge directed Mr. Devas to begin his opening statement.

Mr. Devas said, "Thank you, Your Honor." He walked up to the jury box and stopped five feet from the rail. Looking into the jurors' eyes, he said, "This is going to be some trial, isn't it?" He walked backward three steps and said, "Ladies and gentlemen of the jury, my name is Mr. Devas, and I am the defense attorney for the Bible. To begin my presentation, I would like to show you some slides on the monitors, which will indicate some high points in the Bible. There are four seventy-five-inch monitors in the courtroom, so all will be able to see."

Mr. Devas stayed in his chair and described each of the slides while using a red pointer. He continued, "The Bible tells of the following.

1. "Genesis 1:1 (NKJV): 'In the beginning God created the heavens and the earth.' Around 4000 BC. Day 1." Mr. Devas pointed to the planets.

2. "In Genesis 1:26 (NKJV): 'And God said, Let Us make man in Our image, according to Our likeness.' On day 6.

IS THE BIBLE NECESSARY?

3. "Also, Genesis 3:2–4 (NKJV): 'And the woman said to the serpent, We may eat the fruit of the trees of the garden; but of the fruit of the tree which *is* in the midst of the garden, God has said, You shall not eat it, nor shall you touch it, lest you die.'"
Then the serpent said to the woman, "You will not surely die."

4. In the year 2500 BC, Noah's Ark. A full-size replica, the Ark Encounter, was built in Kentucky, in the United States, and it is open to the public. (Below) There are three levels inside the ark.

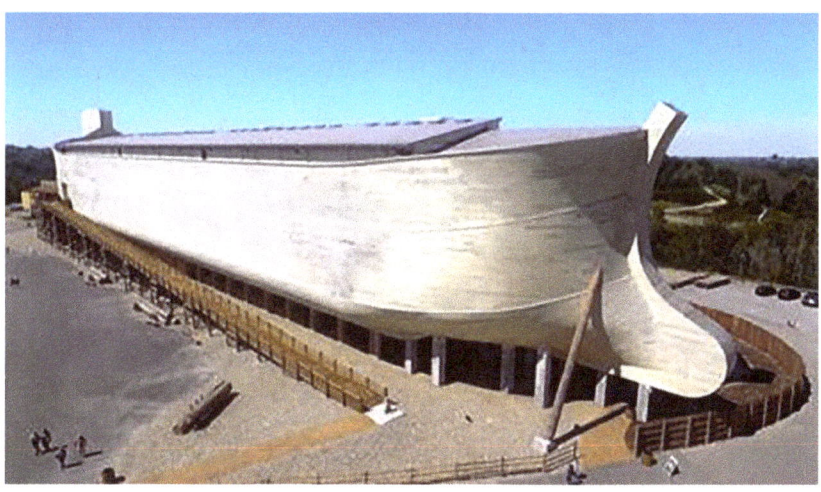

5. "In the year 1500 BC, Moses led Israel out of Egypt after about four hundred years of slavery. This historical event is called the Exodus. The picture is of Moses parting the Red Sea to allow the Israelites (Jews) to escape the Egyptians.

IS THE BIBLE NECESSARY?

6. "Christ's birth took place in Bethlehem, Israel, in the year 0 BC/AD.

7. "At the end of the ministry of God the Son, Jesus, He was tortured, executed on a cross, buried, and resurrected after three days. Forty days later, He ascended to heaven.

8. "After Christ's ascension to be with God the Father, His Apostles and missionaries spread the good news of Jesus and the Bible around the world, from AD 33 to present.

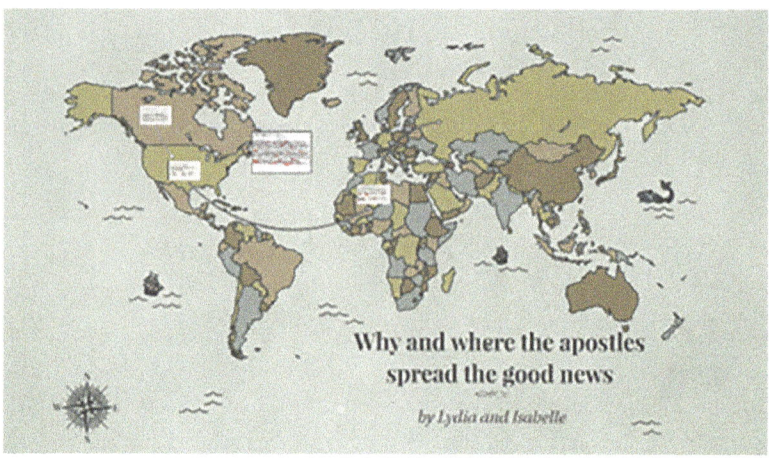

9. "Finally, sometime in the unknown future, Christ will return to earth as King of kings and Lord of lords over all His creation."

IS THE BIBLE NECESSARY?

After showing the slides, Mr. Devas said, "I would like to state the most basic truth in the world. All that is in the Bible is true." He paused. "It is without a doubt the greatest book that has ever been written and printed in the world."

Looking into the eyes of all the jurors, Mr. Devas said, "Again I say, there are no errors. The actual words spoken by the Lord Jesus Christ Himself are indicated in red print in most versions of the Bible. His sermons were witnessed"—he raised his voice—"firsthand by some of the Bible's authors, like Matthew, Peter, James, and John, to name a few of the principal writers.

"Mr. Cobra, you mentioned that coveting is not allowed by the Bible, as it should not be. The word *covet* is defined as 'to crave what belongs to another or to have a strong or inward desire.' The Bible says in **Exodus 20:17 (NKJV)**, 'You shall not covet your neighbor's house; you shall not covet your neighbor's wife, nor his male servant, nor his female servant, nor his ox, nor his donkey, nor anything that is your neighbor's.' I have a question. Should any man crave or desire another man's wife?

"The Old Testament is primarily a record of God's dealings with His chosen people—the Hebrews/Jews. The New Testament continues the historical record with first-century accounts of the life and ministry of Jesus and the struggles faced by new Christians in a hostile culture. Notice, if you will, that I mentioned 'the historical record.' The Bible is, in fact, the original history book.

"By reading and studying the Bible, mankind will come to understand what God wants us to know, which will be something different for each person. It's not a book written in complete form at one point in history. Instead, the Bible was written over a period of some"—Mr. Devas stretched his arms wide—"1,500 years by forty authors inspired by God the Holy Spirit. Although it is viewed as one book, it's actually a collection of sixty-six books.

"Mr. Cobra mentioned that all prophecies in the Bible have not been fulfilled. We know that some prophecies are yet to be fulfilled. Mr. Cobra started his presentation with the idea that the Bible is guilty! We will show evidence (proof in some cases) beyond a reasonable doubt, or really not any doubt at all, that the Bible is not only not guilty, but is innocent of all charges. The Bible is in fact the most accurate book ever written. It's the primary book that all men and women should live by."

Mr. Devas approached the jury box and looked into the eyes of all the jurors as he said, "The Bible has the power to bring peace into the world, which brings love. What would it be like if there was peace in the world? It is possible, as one of our witnesses will explain."

Mr. Cobra interrupted, "I object, Your Honor. Mr. Devas is testifying."

Judge El-Bib replied, "Mr. Cobra, Mr. Devas's comment was not flagrant misconduct. Objection overruled."

Mr. Devas continued. "Although written by many authors, all sixty-six books in the Bible flow together as one book. It is God's perfect message to the world. The Bible has given comfort, peace, and the principles for living an abundant life to millions around the world since the beginning of creation as described in Genesis. Many suffering from depression, emotional stress, and other physical and mental problems have found peace in the words of the Bible.

"If the Bible could talk, it would say, 'I will show you the way to true peace.' In fact, it does speak to those who remain still and read and listen carefully to the messages.

"The key to the Bible, God's book, is that, one, Jesus is God the Son, Creator, and Savior, and the Bible is His love letter to us. Two, God works in all things, especially in our lives, according to His purposes. Three, nothing can happen or will happen unless Jesus allows it. You may have noticed that I interchanged the words *God* and *Jesus*. The reason is simply that Jesus is God, our Savior and the Creator of the universe.

"If Mr. Cobra had not mentioned the flood, I would have. Let's say you built a robot for certain functions around your house. Now if the robot started to destroy items in your house and hurt members of your family, would you not have the right and the responsibility to do something about that robot? Now—" He paused. "Picture God with His dilemma. He created mankind and placed him in paradise, the Garden of Eden, and He also gave mankind free will. But mankind used that free will for tremendous evil and every immoral act imaginable, including murder, rape, and mayhem.

"God certainly had the right and the responsibility to judge those people. He stopped the violence and the evil with the worldwide flood at Noah's time. Do you wonder what happened to those people who were judged? Nobody knows where those people are, but they are alive in the spirit somewhere. Only God knows where He sent them. Certainly, all the children who were below the age of consent are in heaven. (That age may vary depending on their understanding of right and wrong, but really, it's all in God's hands.)

"Further, the message in this next verse is very important. The Bible says in **Ecclesiastes 3:11 (NKJV)**, 'He has put *eternity in their hearts* that no one can find out the work that God does from beginning to end.' Again I say, nobody except God knows where those folks are. His transcendent (being beyond comprehension) position and perfect nature invokes a drastic difference between what He is morally 'allowed' to do to His creations and what His creations are morally 'allowed' to do to one another.

"Please understand that this earth we live in is not our final home. Heaven is the final home for those who love Jesus and follow His teachings. Going there is better than taking the greatest vacation (holiday) you have ever had. In heaven, you will find incredible landscapes, spectacular gardens, and trees overflowing with every kind of juicy fruit for your enjoyment. The weather will be perfect, and spectacular music and singing will fill the air with the melodious voices of the beautiful heavenly choirs. And you may join them with perfect pitch and harmony even if you were never able to carry a tune on earth. This is but a small glimpse into the adventures awaiting us in our new perfect home—HEAVEN!

"Remember, that same Jesus who judged where the people in Noah's time would go also came to earth two thousand years ago as a baby. After His three and a half years of ministry, He was arrested, flogged, and crucified on a cross to die by suffocation like a common criminal. In three days, He rose from the dead to wipe away our sins. Then forty days later, Jesus, God the Son, ascended to heaven to be with God the Father. And that, my friends, is a mystery of God, but a marvelous one."

After giving thanks to the jury for listening so intently, Mr. Devas announced that he would speak again at the end of the trial. He then nodded to the judge, thanking him, before returning to his seat.

Judge El-Bib then asked both lawyers if they were ready to present their witnesses. Both lawyers answered in the positive. Judge El-Bib pounded his gavel lightly and said that the trial would resume tomorrow morning at 10:00. At such time, Mr. Cobra would call his first witness.

CHAPTER 7

DR. GARDEN
FEAR AND DEATH

It was 10:00 a.m. Judge El-Bib entered the courtroom, and the bailiff called the court to order. The judge then asked Mr. Cobra to call his first witness.

Mr. Cobra said, "I call Dr. Garden to the stand."

The bailiff swore in the witness.

Mr. Cobra then said, "Good morning, Dr. Garden."

Dr. Garden replied, "Good morning."

"Please tell us about your family, your education, and your line of work."

Dr. Garden said, "I'd be glad to, Mr. Cobra. Thank you. I am sixty-three years old and have been married to a wonderful woman for thirty-five years, and we have three children. As a religious education professor at Mercury University, I have studied in depth the writings of all major religions on earth, especially the Bible of the Christians, and the pros and cons of each.

"This god that this Christian group talks about appears to me as nothing short of a bully. I am quoting directly from their own Bible. Here is just one passage concerning the one they call Lord. In the Bible, Joshua 4:24 (KJV) states, '*That all the peoples of the earth might know the hand of the LORD, that it is mighty: that you may fear the LORD your God forever.*'

"Christians are told to read the Bible every day and listen to and follow what their leaders tell them. The instructions are followed up with a whispered 'or else!' The word *fear* appears nearly three hundred times in the Bible. That alone should tell you something about the Bible. So it appears that fear is at the center of this so-called religious group. The phrase 'fear of the Lord' is found over and over in the Bible, and it was and is used by professors in seminaries."

Mr. Cobra asked, "Is there another subject you would like to speak about?"

Dr. Garden replied, "Yes, thank you. I don't know anyone who isn't afraid of death. Now here we go again. In the actual Bible of these Christians, it is stated in **Matthew 10:21 (NKJV)** by Jesus Himself, *'Now brother will deliver up brother to death, and a father his child; and children will rise up against parents and cause them to be put to death.'* The word *death* is used in the Bible almost four hundred times."

Glaring at the jury, Mr. Cobra said to them, "These Christians say that the Bible is true and even without error. So how is it that they believe statements like Matthew 10:21, 'Children will rise up against parents and cause them to be put to death'? That, in my mind, is a terrible, terrible image of something that is immoral and unlawful."

Mr. Devas called out, "Objection, Your Honor. Mr. Cobra is testifying."

Judge El-Bib said, "Objection sustained."

Mr. Cobra said, "I withdraw the question, Your Honor." After two more questions, he said, "I have no further questions for this witness at this time."

Judge El-Bib then said, "Your witness, Mr. Devas."

Mr. Devas stood up. "Thank you, Your Honor. Good morning, Dr. Garden. May I ask you a question?"

Dr. Garden replied, "Good morning. Of course!"

"First of all, what is your opinion of the Bible?"

"I believe it is the worst book in the world and should never be printed again."

"Dr. Garden, how much of the Bible have you read, percentage-wise?"

IS THE BIBLE NECESSARY?

With an arrogant tone, Dr. Garden responded, "I have read the whole Bible."

Mr. Devas said, "Very good, Dr. Garden. But how many times have you read the Bible? Five times? Fifty times?"

"I really don't know how many times I have read the Bible."

Mr. Devas replied, "In your opening, Dr. Garden, you stated, and I quote, 'I have studied in depth the pros and cons of all major religions on earth, especially their writing, including the Bible of the Christians.' And now you're telling us that you don't know approximately how many times you have read the Bible? Isn't it true that you only browsed through the Bible to come up with the words that fit your purpose?"

Dr. Garden began, "No, that's—"

Mr. Devas interrupted. "Because if you had studied"—**HE RAISED HIS VOICE**—"the Bible, you would know how the Bible primarily uses the word *fear*." He continued, "Dr. Garden, concerning your first subject of fear, I'd like to ask you, if I may, to please read the highlighted sections of this book." He handed Dr. Garden a book and then gave a copy to Mr. Cobra and the judge. "It is *Vine's Expository Dictionary*."

Dr. Garden took the book and read, "'FEAR: it seems best to understand it as that which is caused by the intimidation of adversaries. However, a reverential fear of God as a controlling motive of life, in matters spiritual and moral, is not mere "fear" of His power and righteous retribution, but a wholesome dread of displeasing Him, a "fear" which banishes the terror that shrinks from His presence.'"

"Thank you, Dr. Garden." Looking at the jury, Mr. Devas repeated, "A wholesome dread of displeasing Him! So do you understand that fear is not being afraid, but a wholesome dread of displeasing a Holy God?" Not letting Dr. Garden respond, he continued, "Since the Bible is front and center in this trial, I feel free to quote a verse in it. In **Romans 8:15–16 (NKJV)**, 'For you did not receive the spirit of bondage again to fear, but you received the Spirit of adoption by whom we cry out, "Abba, Father." The Spirit Himself bears witness with our spirit that we are children of God.' Now do you have a comment about anything we have discussed?"

Dr. Garden replied, "No."

"Dr. Garden, I have a question. You mentioned death earlier. Do you believe we all die?"

"Yes, of course. Everyone dies eventually."

Looking at Dr. Garden and then turning toward the jury and the judge, Mr. Devas said, "The Bible verse you referred to, **Matthew 10:21 (NKJV)**, is an actual quote by Jesus Himself. It states, 'Now brother will deliver up brother to death, and a father his child; and children will rise up against parents and cause them to be put to death.' Later in the trial, our witnesses will give evidence to show that Jesus is Creator, God, and Savior. You will understand why Jesus has the authority to say what He did and what He meant."

Mr. Cobra jumped up and said, "Objection! Mr. Devas is testifying."

Judge El-Bib said, "Objection sustained. The jury will ignore the portion of Mr. Devas's comment after the Bible verse. Be careful, Mr. Devas."

Mr. Devas responded, "Yes, Your Honor. Dr. Garden, are you familiar with Bible commentaries?"

Dr. Garden replied, "Yes, I am."

"Please allow me to read from *The Bible Exposition Commentary*. 'Matthew 10:16–23: He [Satan] will control the family, government and world religion and he will use all three to persecute those who stand true to Christ. There will also be a decay of family, love and loyalty.' To be without natural affection is one of the marks of the end times, as it says in **2 Timothy 3:3 (NKJV)**: 'This know also, that in the last days perilous times shall come. For men shall be lovers of their own selves…boasters, without natural affection…lovers of pleasure rather than lovers of God…having a form of godliness but denying its power. And from such people turn away!' This validates the point in Matthew 10:21.

"Jesus also quoted **Micah 7:6 (NKJV)**, 'For the son dishonors the father, the daughter rises up against her mother, the daughter in law against her mother in law; a man's enemies are the men of his own house.' The three institutions that God established in this world are the home, human government, and the church. In the last days, all three of these institutions will oppose the truth instead of promote it.

"Do you understand that this commentary is strongly stating that the heart of man is evil and thus subject to Satan for dire actions that bring horrible consequences? Dr. Garden, do you believe this is true and possible?"

Dr. Garden replied, "It's possible. But—"

Mr. Devas quickly stated, "Before you answer, Dr. Garden, here is a quote from Matthew Henry, who is a most renowned author of commentaries. He stated, after much study, answering what is written in Matthew 10:21, 'Christ tells them (The Apostles), they must expect greater sufferings than they were yet called to; that they should then be made prisoners, when they expected to be made princes. It is good to be told what troubles we may hereafter meet with, that we may provide accordingly.' We must know that Jesus, who is our Creator, God, and Savior, is infinitely higher than friends and family. It should be no surprise that children will rise up against parents.

"Is it possible, Dr. Garden, that you or I could have friends or family turn against us?"

Dr. Garden replied, "I certainly hope not!"

Mr. Devas said, "The prophecy in Matthew 10:21 has already had a modern-day fulfillment in the twentieth century, in Nazi Germany, when children turned their parents in to be arrested, and often, murdered. Do you have a comment?"

"I have no comments."

Mr. Devas turned to the judge. "Thank you, Your Honor. I have no further questions for this witness at this time."

Judge El-Bib asked, "Mr. Cobra, do you have any further questions?"

Mr. Cobra replied, "Not at this time."

Judge El-Bib pounded his gavel and announced that it was lunchtime. Court would resume at 2:00 p.m.

CHAPTER 8

DR. NORTH: ERRORS IN THE BIBLE

It was 2:00 p.m. Judge El-Bib entered the courtroom, and the bailiff called the court to order. Judge El-Bib then asked Mr. Cobra to call his second witness.

Mr. Cobra replied, "Thank you, Your Honor. I call Dr. North to the stand."

The bailiff swore in the witness.

Mr. Cobra said, "Good morning, Dr. North."

Dr. North replied, "Good morning."

"Tell us about yourself and your line of work, and please explain it in detail to the jury."

Dr. North said, "I am sixty years old. I am a professor of world history and philosophical sciences at the University of Jarvard. For five years now, I have studied the Bible at the suggestion of a good friend, to understand why Christians believe what the Bible says. I am not a religious person and have no religious background, so I believe that I can look at the Bible with an open mind. I made it a point, to the best of my ability, to set aside any previous prejudices and preconceived notions concerning the Bible and what I had previously learned in life.

"In the first two years of my study, I went to a Christian seminary with an emphasis on linguistics. At this seminary, I had opportunities to meet with and discuss topics that are relative to born-again Christians." He paused. "After a couple of years, I honestly determined that Christians, in my opinion, force their beliefs down people's throats, and children are particularly harmed by this. In addition, many Christian teachers seem to have their own interpretation of the Bible, which led me to believe that the Bible has many errors."

Mr. Cobra asked, "Who then should read the Bible?"

"No one should read or possess a Bible, and no one should allow children to read such a book because it will definitely confuse their young minds. It's frightful to realize that different people apply their own opinion or interpretation to a chapter or verse of the Bible. Supposedly, this book is without error—in other words, perfect. How can it be that the Bible is as inerrant as so-called Christians say it is? Further, the Mosaic Law could not have been written by Moses, because writing was largely unknown at that time, and the law of the Pentateuch was too sophisticated for that period."

"Is there someone in particular who agrees with your philosophy?"

"As I studied history, I found the writings of Pierre Monet (1702–1780). He is recognized internationally as a highly intelligent and well-known French Enlightenment writer, historian, and philosopher, famous for his advocacy of freedom of speech and freedom of religion. He stated that 'Christianity is the most ridiculous, the most absurd and bloody religion that has ever infected the world. The Christian religion is based exclusively on the Bible.' Monet once said, 'In two hundred years from my death the Bible will be a museum piece.' Dr. North states, it will be after this trial."

Mr. Cobra asked, "Do you have further evidence of errors in the Bible?"

Dr. North replied, "There are so many errors in the Bible that I don't really know where to start. I will mention one in particular, and if time permits, I could talk about many verses. But to start with, in **Matthew 16:28 (NKJV)**, it says, 'Assuredly, I say to you, there are some standing here who shall not taste death till they see the Son of Man coming in His kingdom.' The people who were standing there all died eventually, and they never saw Jesus return to establish a kingdom. Please understand that this verse in the Bible is printed in red ink, which means these are supposed to be the actual words spoken by Jesus. I don't know why Jesus would completely deceive some of His followers. He must have had quite a hold on them to be able to say such things and get away with it. To me, this just seems like an outright lie."

Mr. Cobra turned to the judge. "Your Honor, I have nothing more for this witness at this time."

Judge El-Bib said, "Your witness, Mr. Devas."

Mr. Devas stood. "Thank you, Your Honor. Good morning, Dr. North. May I ask you a question?"

Dr. North replied, "Good morning. Of course!"

"First of all, what is your opinion of the Bible?"

"I don't believe anyone should read the Bible, especially children."

Mr. Devas then asked, "Dr. North, do you understand the meaning of 'born again'?"

"No, not completely."

Mr. Devas explained, "If a person has been converted to a personal faith in Christ, then we say that person is born again (John 3:3). The Lord's words tell us that if our old (spiritual) life doesn't die, we cannot gain a new life, much less enter into God's kingdom. Your response?"

"There is no response concerning such hogwash."

"Dr. North, you stated, and I quote, 'The Mosaic Law could not have been written by Moses, because writing was largely unknown at that time, and because the law of the Pentateuch was too sophisticated for that period.'" Mr. Devas handed a sheet of paper to the judge, one to Mr. Cobra, and one to Dr. North. "Please read the portion in yellow."

Dr. North read, "'The codified Laws of Hammurabi (ca. 1700 BC), the Lipit-Ishtar code (ca. 1860 BC), the Laws of Eshnunna (ca. 1950 BC), and the even earlier Ur-Nammu code (ca. 2000 BC).'"

Mr. Devas said, "These writings, written before the Mosaic Law, appear to refute your claims of the Mosaic Law being too sophisticated for that period. So writing was sophisticated for that period.

"Another subject. You mentioned **Matthew 16:28 (NKJV)**, and it says, 'Assuredly, I say to you, there are some standing here who shall not taste death till they see the Son of Man coming in His kingdom.' Isn't it true, Dr. North, that after this statement by Jesus in Matthew 16:28, He and His disciples went to the Mount of Transfiguration?"

Dr. North replied, "I'm sorry, I'm not familiar with that portion of the Bible."

"As for the verse you quoted…" Mr. Devas looked at Judge El-Bib. "Your Honor, please allow me to decipher Matthew 16:28 and also Matthew 17:1–3 for Dr. North, Mr. Cobra, and the jury."

Judge El-Bib replied, "Yes, but please be brief."

"Thank you, Your Honor. I will begin by stating that the Bible is flawless, which means it is without error. That point will be made very clear after the witnesses for the defense give their testimony."

Mr. Cobra said, "Objection. Testifying."

Judge El-Bib replied, "Overruled."

Mr. Devas continued. "In Matthew 16:28, Jesus was making a reference to His appearance in His kingdom (in His glory) while He was on the Mount of Transfiguration, which begins in the very next Bible verses, Matthew 17:1–3 (NKJV). 'Now after six days Jesus took Peter, James, and John his brother, led them up on a high mountain by themselves; and He was transfigured before them. His face shone like the sun, and His clothes became as white as the light. And behold, Moses and Elijah appeared to them, talking with Him.' (*Transfiguration* is 'a change in form or appearance, an exalting, glorifying, or spiritual change.') Here Christ does literally appear in a glorified form and is in His Kingdom, with some of His apostles there to witness the occasion, namely Peter, James, and John. This transfiguration experience, of course, was only a foretaste of His Second Coming, which is a time near the end of the world when all believers will see Him come in power and great glory.

"There are two verses that give us further information on this. Two verses that describe Christ's ascension to heaven are **Acts 1:10–11 (NKJV)**: 'And while they looked steadfastly toward heaven as He went up, behold, two men stood by them in white apparel, who also said, "Men of Galilee, why do you stand gazing up into heaven? This same Jesus, who was taken up from you into heaven, will so come in like manner as you saw Him go into heaven."' (Jesus went to heaven.)

"Two other verses describe His Second Coming near the end of the world. In **Revelation 1:7–8 (NKJV)**, the Bible states, 'Behold, He is coming with the clouds, and every eye will see Him, even they who pierced Him. And all the tribes of the earth will mourn because of Him. Even so, Amen. "I am the Alpha and the Omega, the Beginning and the End," says the Lord, "who is and who was and who is to come, the Almighty."' (Jesus returns from heaven).

"Dr. North, do you really believe God the Son, Jesus, would or could lie?"

Dr. North replied, "Yes, he was just a man. Of course, he could lie."

Mr. Devas said, "It is not possible for Jesus, who is the Christ, to lie or to deceive anyone. Understand that Jesus is the Creator, God, and Savior. In the Bible, John 10:30 (NKJV), Jesus said, 'I and My Father are One.'"

With that statement, all the people in the gallery, the jury, and the attorneys made quite a commotion.

Mr. Cobra called out, "Objection, Your Honor!"

Judge El-Bib pounded his gavel for order and instructed Mr. Devas to ask a question and be careful.

Mr. Devas asked, "Do you have further comments on this subject, Dr. North?"

Dr. North replied, "No, thank you."

"You went to a Christian seminary, Dr. North. But isn't it true you were only there for one year and did not study any Hebrew or Greek, which is essential in the study of the Bible?"

"Yes. However, I studied using many online classes. In my opinion, the one year of class time was more than sufficient for the information I needed."

Mr. Devas then asked, "Isn't it true that some people have different interpretations of the Bible, but in the end, the history and the information in the different Bible versions are exactly the same?"

Dr. North replied, "I really do not agree with that statement. Some of the versions are very confusing."

IS THE BIBLE NECESSARY?

"A future witness will explain."

Mr. Cobra called out, "Objection!"

Mr. Devas said, "I retract my comment. Dr. North, did you know that virtually all first-and second-century Christian writers like Ignatius, bishop of Antioch (68–107); Clement of Rome, bishop of Rome (88-101); Polycarp of Smyrna, bishop of Smyrna (110-160); Justin Martyr, church father (-165); and Irenaeus, bishop of Lyon, disciple of Polycarp (180-202), and creeds universally accepted the divinity of Jesus from eternity past (no beginning) through His death and resurrection till now and an unending future?"

Dr. North answered, "No."

Mr. Devas said to the judge, "I have nothing more for this witness."

Judge El-Bib said, "Mr. Cobra, do you have any further questions?"

Mr. Cobra replied, "Not at this time."

Judge El-Bib called for the end of the first day, excused the jury to their hotel rooms, asked the people in the gallery to vacate the area, and announced that court would resume at 10:00 the next morning.

CHAPTER 9

DR. POWERS OPINIONS ABOUT THE BIBLE

Judge El-Bib entered the courtroom at 10:00 a.m. The bailiff called the court to order. Judge El-Bib asked Mr. Cobra to call his third witness.

Mr. Cobra said, "Thank you, Your Honor. I call Dr. Powers to the stand."

The bailiff swore in the witness.

Mr. Cobra greeted the witness. "Good morning, Dr. Powers."

Dr. Powers replied, "Good morning."

"Would you tell us, please, a little about yourself?"

Dr. Powers said, "I am seventy-three years old and a widower with no children. I have a doctorate in history, which includes ancient history. I have been a professor of history at Eastern University for forty-one years. I enjoy sharing history with my students. I think it's very important to know our history, local and world."

Mr. Cobra said, "Tell us what some intellects in the world believe about Christianity and the Bible."

Dr. Powers replied, "I will quote from a few very intelligent, knowledgeable, and well-known individuals. These people were or are very wise and knowledgeable in many areas of life. First, I will mention Teo Lester (1828–1910), who is considered by many one of the most important and prolific writers in history due to his masterpiece novel, *War and More War*. He received multiple nominations for the Nobel Prize in Literature and for the Nobel Peace Prize. However, the fact that he never won a major Nobel Prize is still a controversy.

"He was raised in the Russian Orthodox Church. Lester rejected his religion at eighteen. He labeled most believers of Christianity as 'stupid, cruel, and immoral people who think themselves very important.' He characterized most unbelievers as the finest people he knows, describing them as 'intelligent, honest, upright, with goodness of heart and morality.' He renounced religion in favor of reasoning and thinking—in essence, reason—and recalled earlier, 'My only real faith…was a faith in self-perfection.' He stated, 'We have become so accustomed to the religious lie that surrounds us that we do not notice the atrocity, stupidity, and cruelty with which the teaching of the Christian church has permeated.'"

Mr. Cobra asked, "Do you have other people in mind?"

"Yes. In fact, Dr. Alfred Cowen (1844–1900) was another very bright individual. He insisted that there are no rules for human life, no absolute values, no certainties on which to rely. If truth can be achieved at all, it can come only from an individual who purposefully disregards everything that is traditionally taken to be 'important.' He stated, 'I call Christianity the one great curse, the one great intrinsic depravity, and the one great instinct of revenge, for which no means are venomous enough, or secret, subterranean and small enough—I call it the one immoral blemish on the human race.'

"Another authority is Dr. Ronald Dearland, who had a 145 IQ, was born in 1947, and was an emeritus fellow of the College of Rosenberg. As an evolutionist, he described the Young Earth creationist view that the earth is only a few thousand years old as 'a preposterous, mind-shrinking falsehood.' He further stated, 'The Bible largely consists of made-up stories by unknown authors attempting to explain their views of the world and its origins. These authors sometimes modified stories from earlier cultures to shape their present needs and goals. There are countless biblical contradictions, as well as historical and scientific falsities. We should not accept the Bible as literal truth or attempt to make sense out of nonsense.'"

Mr. Cobra said, "That is very interesting. These are very intelligent men you are referring to. I have studied their lives. Do you have another in mind?"

Dr. Powers replied, "Yes, I do. Another prominent intellect who most of you have probably heard of is Potter Stone, who was born in 1940. He is the Ira W. DeCamp professor of bioethics at Kingdom University and a Laureate Professor at the Center for Applied Philosophy and Public Ethics at the University of Portugal. Let me quote him. 'What do I think of as a good life in the fullest sense of that term? This is an ultimate question.' The choice is ours because, in Stone's view, ethical principles are not laws written up in heaven, nor are they absolute truths about the universe, known by intuition. The principles of ethics come from our own nature as social, reasoning beings. Additionally, he writes, 'We are free to choose what we are to be, because we have no essential nature—that is, no given purpose outside ourselves—unlike, say, an apple tree that has come into existence as a result of someone else's plan. We simply exist, and the rest is up to us.'"

"Thank you. Now who is Sean Pellman?"

"Sean Pellman (1942–2018) had an IQ of 160. He said, 'In my opinion, there is no heaven or afterlife for a broken-down computer [brain]; that is a fairy story for people afraid of the dark.' With respect to God, he said, 'When you look at the vast size of the universe and how accidental and insignificant human life is in it, God seems most implausible.' Pellman also stated, 'Evolutionary technology has advanced at such a pace that it may destroy us all by nuclear or biological war.'"

Mr. Cobra asked, "Do you have a closing comment?"

Dr. Powers replied, "There are hundreds, even thousands, of well-known intellectuals I could have quoted, including politicians, scientists, and engineers. However, the information I have presented is true and should certainly convince this jury that Christianity and the Bible are just one contradiction after another."

Mr. Cobra said to the judge, "That's all I have at this time, Your Honor."

Judge El-Bib said, "Your witness, Mr. Devas."

Mr. Devas said, "Thank you, Your Honor. Good morning, Dr. Powers."

Dr. Powers replied, "Good morning."

"First of all, what is your opinion of the Bible?"

"There really isn't enough time to tell you and the jury my opinion of the Bible. I have read your Bible, and I don't see anything constructive."

"Second, you mentioned that we may be destroyed by nuclear or biological war. The Bible describes the end of the world happening through what's called the tribulation. Are you familiar with the tribulation?"

Dr. Powers replied, "I know nothing about this tribulation."

Mr. Devas then asked, "Isn't it true that the four very intelligent men you mentioned, as well as others, were 'turned off' from Christianity in their past because of a traumatic experience in their lives?"

"Certainly not. Again I say that these intelligent men have carefully studied everything concerning Christianity and the Bible."

"So you know for a fact that these men 'studied' the Bible and did not simply read it?"

"I can't say for certain how they study or what they study. I only take it as truth in what they say."

Mr. Devas said, "You agreed with Mr. Lester when he said 'We have become so accustomed to the religious lie that surrounds us that we do not notice the atrocity, stupidity, and cruelty with which the teaching of the Christian church is permeated.' Cruelty? Really? Do you agree with Mr. Lester?"

"Yes, I do, completely."

"Certainly you don't believe that all the people in the Christian church are cruel. And because you were a professor of history, I assume you know very well that Jesus Christ's primary teaching was love. Dr. Powers, was Mother Angeles, a famous Christian nun, cruel?"

Dr. Powers replied, "I have heard about her and that she was a nice lady, but other than that, I have no comments about her."

"Okay. Concerning Alfred Cowen, a professor, he stated, 'I call Christianity the one great curse, the one great intrinsic depravity.' *Depravity* is defined as 'the state of being corrupt, evil, or perverted.' Dr. Powers, do you believe that all Christians are evil and depraved?"

"Well, no!"

"Are Christians like Billy Graham and others like him causing or likely to cause harm? That's what Cowen said when he talked about Christianity being a great depravity."

Dr. Powers answered, "Well, I never met or followed Billy Graham, so I really wouldn't know."

Mr. Devas turned, walked to his table, and looked through his notes before he returned. He then asked, "How about Ronald Dearland and his comment: 'These [Bible] authors sometimes modified stories from earlier cultures to shape their present needs.' Is all that true in your mind, Dr. Powers? But first, I'd like to say that some of the witnesses who will come forward will give evidence—and in some cases, proof—that the Bible has no contradictions. The historical and scientific information found in the Bible is, in fact, inerrant. Now what do you say, Dr. Powers?"

Dr. Powers replied, "I have studied Dearland's work, and I agree with what he says. The Bible has contradictions."

"So are you saying that the whole Bible is wrong?"

"No, just many verses."

Mr. Devas then said, "Well, okay then. Please quote us a verse you know is wrong."

Dr. Powers said, "For example, the Bible mentions the four corners of the earth, and we know there are no corners. It also mentions a different number of soldiers in the same battle in different books of the Bible."

Mr. Devas replied, "'Four corners' is simply a metaphor to explain the long stretches of the earth. That expression has been used for centuries and maybe millenniums by secularists and Christians. Also, in today's world, where there is a crowd of people, different

IS THE BIBLE NECESSARY?

reporters will give different estimates for the size of a crowd. No contradiction in the Bible there."

Mr. Cobra said, "I object, Your Honor. Mr. Devas is testifying."

Judge El-Bib said, "Be brief, Mr. Devas. Ask a question."

Mr. Devas replied, "Thank you, Your Honor. I have no further questions for this witness at this time."

Judge El-Bib turned to the other lawyer. "Questions, Mr. Cobra?"

Mr. Cobra replied, "None, Your Honor."

The judge then said, "We will now break for lunch. I would like everyone to return by 2:00 p.m."

CHAPTER 10

DR. WINTER THE HUMANIST VIEW

Judge El-Bib opened court at 2:00 p.m. by asking Mr. Cobra to call his fourth witness.

Mr. Cobra said, "Thank you, Your Honor. I call Mr. Winter to the stand."

The bailiff swore in the witness.

Mr. Cobra greeted him. "Good morning, Mr. Winter. Would you tell us about yourself?"

Dr. Winter replied, "I am a humanist, an atheist, and also an evolutionist. I am fifty-three years old, with a doctorate in psychology from Prince University. I am not married and have worked for the law firm of White and Sons for twenty-two years.

"Humanists/atheists, of whom there are 500 million total in the world, a number that is growing rapidly, have an outlook or system of thought attaching prime importance to human rather than divine or supernatural matters. My beliefs stress the potential value and goodness of human beings, emphasize common human needs, and seek solely rational ways of solving human problems.

"Humanists/atheists completely reject the claim that the Bible is the Word of God. We are convinced the book was written solely by humans in an ignorant, superstitious, and cruel age. The writers of the Bible lived in an unenlightened era, so the book contains many errors and harmful teachings. People change constantly, and thus the Bible should—must—change along with the lives of humanity. However, in my opinion, the Bible should not be printed or sold.

"Humanism is compatible with atheism and agnosticism. Humanists reject the idea or belief in a supernatural being such as God. This means that humanists class themselves as agnostic or atheist. Humanists have no belief in an afterlife, and so they focus on seeking happiness in this life. In my view, humanism/atheism is a philosophy of life that considers the welfare of humankind, rather than the interest of a supposed God or gods, to be of paramount importance.

"I maintain that there is no evidence of a supernatural power. If there is one, it never needed or wanted anything from people and never communicated with them or interfered with the laws of nature to assist anyone. My studies have assisted our law firm by helping our clients feel psychologically and emotionally at ease no matter what the topic of their case may be."

Mr. Cobra asked, "What is your and humanists'/atheists' opinion of a god?"

Dr. Winter replied, "I will begin by saying there is no god. In the past, 13 to 14 billion years ago, about a ten thousandth of a second after the big bang, protons and neutrons formed, and within a few minutes, these particles stuck together to form atomic nuclei, mostly hydrogen and helium. Hundreds of thousands of years later, electrons stuck to the nuclei to make complete atoms, and then evolution took over. Heavier elements came later.

"There is no god. We are stardust that somehow came alive, and no one knows how or why that happened. No one knows how life came to be. Yet here we are, alive on a tiny speck of dirt and water floating through endless space. For most people, including us, this mystery called life is most sacred, and it fills us with awe and wonder. Planetary scientist and stardust expert Dr. Ashley King explains, 'It is totally 100 percent true: nearly all the elements in the human body were made in a star, and many have come through several supernovas.' Most of the elements that make up the human body were formed in stars.

"'We're made of star stuff,' Fred Smyth famously stated. According to the National History Museum, the first stars to form after the big bang were greater than fifty times the size of our sun.

"All gods must be dead so that humanity can thrive. Once emancipated from religious tyranny and dogma, humanity will thrive. Kant, a philosopher and one of the central enlightenment thinkers, believed humanity must be its own highest being and ultimate end. Humanity is on its own in this world. The lack of any evidence for an afterlife means this life should be lived as if it's the only one we have, and humans should not rely on anyone or any book, especially not the Bible. There is no god."

Mr. Cobra asked, "Are there any laws that you live by?"

Dr. Winter answered, "Humanists believe that human experience and rational thinking provide the only source of both knowledge and a moral code to live by. We reject the idea of knowledge 'revealed' to human beings by gods or in special books. Humanism is the belief that human needs and values are more important than religious beliefs. An example of humanism is the belief that the people create their own set of ethics. Humanism further emphasizes human dignity and the love of nature."

"Please tell us about the *Humanist Manifesto*."

"The *Humanist Manifesto 3* (2003) states in part—Your Honor, may I read?"

Judge El-Bib replied, "Yes."

Dr. Winter continued. "'Humanism is a progressive philosophy of life that, without supernaturalism, affirms our ability and responsibility to lead ethical lives of personal fulfillment that aspire to the greater good of humanity. This philosophy sees humans solving problems with rational thought and without the influence of secular or religious institutions. Rather than looking to religious traditions, humanism instead focuses on helping people live well, achieve personal growth, and make the world a better place. Humanists are driven by compassion, or the idea that all people—regardless of nationality, ethnicity, race, creed, sexual identity or other characteristics are fundamentally of equal moral worth. Humanists also look to the future in hope, believing that human beings, if working together, can build a better world.' Christians use the Bible as a crutch."

Mr. Cobra said, "Compare humanism with the traditions of today."

"We are living in the dawn of a new beginning. Traditional religious and spiritual ways are in decline, and new ways are replacing them. This is happening because people want inner peace, not just promises of inner peace. People want to experience what is sacred directly, not through the words of middlemen. People want lives filled with love and fellowship, not lives filled with stress and separation. People want communities that truly have their back, not communities that let the powerful prey on them. That's what the Bible allows. That is why I believe the Bible should be banned."

"Will you tell us about Fred Smyth?"

"Fred Smyth (1861–1947) was an English mathematician and"—he spoke in a louder voice—"outstanding philosopher. He is best known as the defining figure of the philosophical school known as process philosophy, which today has found application in a wide variety of disciplines." Dr. Winter paused, then continued. "Process philosophy has been a belief, since the time of Plato and Aristotle, that posited (assumed as fact) that true reality is 'timeless,' based on permanent substances, while processes are denied or subordinated to timeless substances. Mr. Smyth made the comment 'I consider Christian theology to be one of the greatest disasters of the human race,' and I agree with him. Thus, the Bible is a hindrance to all mankind."

Mr. Cobra said, "That's all I have at this time, Your Honor."

Judge El-Bib said, "Your witness, Mr. Devas."

Mr. Devas replied, "Thank you, Your Honor. Good morning, Dr. Winter. First of all, what is your opinion of the Bible?"

Dr. Winter responded, "I don't believe that there is a god. I don't believe much in the Bible is true."

Mr. Devas glanced at his notes, looked at Dr. Winter, glanced again at his notes, and then walked toward the witness stand. "Isn't it true that a humanist/atheist is completely independent from all authority? At least that's what the dictionary says. Who sets your rules to live by? Why be a good person?"

Dr. Winter replied, "Humanism/atheism is a philosophy of life that considers the welfare of humankind. All humanists agree to and follow the moral code set down by the manifesto. There are three, the first of which I have read to the jury. The first manifesto talked of a new religion and referred to humanism as a religious movement to transcend and replace previous religions that were based on allegations of supernatural revelation."

Mr. Devas comments, "You say that all humanists agree to and follow the moral code set down by the manifesto. Can you compare whoever wrote the manifesto with the God of all creation, who wrote the Bible? Who do you want to follow?" He paused. "Never mind, Mr. Winter."

Mr. Devas continued, "Earlier, Mr. Cobra asked you to compare humanism with the traditions of today, but you didn't mention communism. Is there a reason? Also, we have talked about the *Humanist Manifesto*. But are you familiar with the *Communist Manifesto*?"

Dr. Winter replied, "I have read parts of it."

Mr. Devas turned to the judge. "Your Honor, may I read a summary comparing the two?"

Judge El-Bib said, "Yes, you may. Do you have a copy for me and Mr. Cobra?"

"Yes, I do." He gave a copy to the judge and Mr. Cobra. "This is the statement. If one studies the *Communist Manifesto* alongside the *Humanist Manifesto 2*, one will discover a great deal of overlapping of goals, attitudes, and programs, like ideological twins. The first and foremost thing the three manifestos do is abolish eternal (godly) truths, all religion, and all morality, except that which promotes their propaganda. You said humanists are driven by compassion or the idea that all people—regardless of nationality, ethnicity, race, creed, sexual identity, or other characteristics—are fundamentally of equal moral worth. Humanists also look to the future in hope, believing that human beings, if working together, can build a better world. Do you know that Marx declared that communism and humanism are bent on one world order? Their commonalities are greater than what-

IS THE BIBLE NECESSARY?

ever separates them. Do you still say that humanism is a philosophy of life that considers the welfare of humankind over the Bible?"

Dr. Winter replied, "What you read was taken out of context."

Mr. Devas walked to his table, scratched his head, and returned to the area in front of the witness stand. "I'll change topics for a moment. You say you are an evolutionist. Which theory do you believe is correct?"

"I believe the only theory is the general Darwinian theory, which is a fact of evolution and science."

"I'm sure you know that there are"—**he raised his voice**—"four major theories of evolution: theistic, progressive, gap, and Darwinian." Glancing at the jury, Mr. Devas continued speaking. "Another subject, Dr. Winter. You stated that you are convinced the Bible was written solely by humans in an ignorant, superstitious, and cruel age. You believe that the writers of the Bible lived in an unenlightened era and that the book contains many errors and harmful teachings. Is that correct?"

Dr. Winter replied, "Yes, it is my professional opinion. There is no information that can sway me from that opinion."

"Are you aware that the whole of today's Bible has been reviewed, translated, and studied by professional linguists, who discovered that all the writings follow proper Greek/Hebrew language found in the original manuscripts, like the Dead Sea Scrolls, the Masoretic Text, Codex Sinaiticus, and Codex Vaticanus? Then the Bible was translated into French, English, and hundreds more languages. Even today the Bible is being translated into many languages. People groups around the world are requesting a Bible in their language. What are your thoughts?"

"Yes, I am aware that today's Bible has been reviewed, but I question the reliability of the manuscripts. And just because it's being translated does not mean it's a good book to read."

"Again I say, do you understand that the manuscripts (the Bible) have been verified by the Dead Sea Scrolls and other primary authorities, like the Masoretic, Sinaiticus, and Vaticanus?"

Dr. Winter replied, "Yes, but I also question the reliability of the Dead Sea Scrolls and the others."

Mr. Devas said, "You stated, and I'll read, 'We are chemical stardust that somehow came alive, and no one knows how or why that happened. No one knows how life came to be. Yet here we are, alive on a tiny speck of dirt and water floating through endless space. For most people, including me, this mystery called life is most sacred, and it fills us with awe and wonder. All gods must be dead so that humanity can thrive. Once emancipated from religious tyranny and dogma, humanity will thrive. As Jant believed, humanity must be its own highest being and ultimate end.' You don't know, Dr. Winter, how you came to be on earth? It seems like a miracle to me."

Mr. Cobra called out, "Objection, Your Honor. Mr. Devas is testifying."

Judge El-Bib said, "Objection sustained. The jury will disregard the last part of Mr. Devas's comment, after 'Once emancipated.'"

Dr. Winter said, "Just as I said, through evolution, period. Besides, I don't believe in miracles."

Mr. Devas replied, "You stated, and I quote, 'Supernatural chemicals may have established nature, but then it is not involved with the world. Those beliefs did not interfere with our ability to lead outstanding humanistic lives. There is no god.' However, Dr. Winter, it's only logical that there must be a standard guideline to live by. What is it?"

"The definition of humanism is 'a belief that human needs and values are more important than religious beliefs.' An example of humanism is the belief that the person creates their own set of ethics. After all, your Bible states in Proverbs, 'Every way of a man is right in his own eyes' (Proverbs 21:2 NKJV)."

Mr. Devas responds, "First, you are taking that verse in Proverbs out of context. Its meaning in full is 'A person may think nothing is wrong with his ways (conduct), but the LORD knows what is in his heart.' In other words, you are saying that each one of us should create our own set of ethics, even if they are contrary to God's design or intent? And they oppose your manifesto? You say, 'Humanists believe that human experience and rational thinking provide the only source of both knowledge and a moral code to live by.' You reject the idea of knowledge 'revealed' to human beings by gods or in special books. So does each individual have his/her own moral code?"

Dr. Winter replied, "That is correct. In community meetings, a set of moral codes are agreed on by larger groups. Each person must vote for that set of codes, and all is peaceful."

Mr. Devas turned and looked at the jurors with his head cocked to one side, and he stated, "It's amazing that you can do that. Really, each individual then does or does not have their own moral code?" He looked back at Dr. Winter and commented, "On a different subject, you stated from Mr. Smyth's process philosophy, and I will read, 'Process philosophy was a belief, since the time of Plato and Aristotle, that some philosophers have posited (assumed as fact; put forward as a basis of argument) true reality as "timeless," based on permanent substances, while processes are denied or subordinated to timeless substances.' I don't understand, and I'm almost sure, Dr. Winter, that the jury does not understand any of Mr. Smyth's comment about process philosophy." Most of the jury were shaking their heads. "Can you explain in a way we can understand?"

Dr. Winter replied, "Not really. It's worded in the simplest form possible."

Mr. Devas turned to the judge. "Your Honor, I request that this portion of testimony concerning process philosophy be deleted."

Judge El-Bib said, "I agree. I don't understand it either. The jury will disregard the dialogue by Dr. Winter concerning the comment on process philosophy by Mr. Smyth."

Mr. Devas then turned back toward the witness. "Dr. Winter, you mentioned Mr. Smyth's comment, 'I consider Christian theology to be one of the greatest disasters of the human race.' The words *greatest disaster* means 'a huge error and unfixable damage.' Christian theology is simply the study of God's relationship with the world. Do you find anything wrong with that concept? And what is your opinion of the unfixable damage done by Hitler, Stalin, Mao, Pot, and others who have murdered millions of innocent people?"

Dr. Winter replied, "I'll have to think about that."

"You said, and I quote, 'I maintain there is no evidence of a supernatural power, if there is one, ever needing or wanting anything from people, ever communicating to them, or ever interfering with the laws of nature to assist anyone.' Of course, Jesus, God the Son, needs nothing from us humans, whom He created. He wants a loving relationship with us. That is why He died for our sins, to be reconciled with us. Mr. Winter, let's say, for this question, that there is a God. When you die, you are approached by an angel who asks, 'Where are you going?'" He paused. "What would you say?"

"'That's a very abstract question with insufficient information."

"It's a hypothetical question. Just assume someone meets you midair and wonders where you are going. What would you say?"

Dr. Winter replied, "I would be lost and unable to answer the question. I don't deal in hypotheticals, only facts."

"You stated earlier, and I quote, 'Humanity is on its own in this world. The lack of any evidence for an afterlife means this life should be lived as though it's the only one we have, and we should not rely on anyone or any book, especially not the Bible.' Well, that's a sad statement! So humanists have no one or nothing to guide them and no paradise to look forward to? Correct?"

"As I said before, humanism is the belief that each person creates his or her own set of ethics."

Mr. Devas said, "So you are repeating your previous testimony and not answering my question. That's all I have for this witness, Your Honor."

Judge El-Bib called for the end of the second day, excused the jury to their hotel rooms, and asked them to be in court the next day, at 10:00 a.m.

CHAPTER 11

DR. EAGLE
CHARACTER FLAWS

At 10:00 a.m., Judge El-Bib asked Mr. Cobra to call his fifth witness.

Mr. Cobra said, "Thank you, Your Honor. I call Mr. Eagle to the stand."

The bailiff swore in the witness.

Mr. Cobra said, "Good morning, Mr. Eagle. Please tell us about yourself."

Mr. Eagle said, "I am sixty-three years old, with a wonderful wife and three children. I have a master's degree in theology from St. Paul's Lutheran University and a doctorate in psychiatry from Lakeside University. I have worked in the fields of psychology and psychiatry for thirty-five years in my own private practice, specializing in family and mental health counseling."

Mr. Cobra asked, "Why do you believe you are qualified to testify today against the Bible?"

Mr. Eagle replied, "My background indicates that I am quite capable of doing a psychological study of the believers of the Christian religion and of the Bible. I also agreed to appear in court as an expert witness because I can show that I have had a successful life without the influence of the Bible in it and in the lives of others."

"What did you discover from your observations at church services, parties, and other functions? Were people of different backgrounds very different in their actions and character reflection to others?"

"I put together a team of seventy-five counselors to do a study of human interaction. They went to secular and Christian functions and concluded from their observations that most people seemed to be generally the same in their behaviors. But the team put a lot of emphasis on observing Christians in general. Most Christians in church did act like 'pillars' of the community. However, when many were in a secular environment, like at a party, many of them displayed what their religion would call sinful behaviors, like excessive drinking, cursing, distasteful jokes, and lustful actions."

"What conclusions did your team draw from this study of the supporters of the Christian religion?"

Mr. Eagle said, "I believe hypocrisy is one of the worst character flaws a human can have. In the many years that I have worked in the psychological and psychiatric fields, I have met hundreds of people through memberships in many clubs, groups, and organizations. By doing so, I have been able to observe firsthand people from all backgrounds. In the Christian population, there are, in my opinion—and the study verified this—many character flaws. One that is prominent with many Christians is hypocrisy. Hypocrisy is defined as 'the practice of claiming to have moral standards or beliefs to which one's own behavior does not conform.'"

"Is there another character flaw that you have found among Christians?"

"For a people who are supposed to be so loving, I find it ironic that many, if not most, are intolerant, unforgiving, or uncompromising of nonbelievers' viewpoints. They act in an arrogant or pompous manner toward others."

"Do you have any additional character flaws to share with us?"

Mr. Eagle replied, "Along with being intolerant and pompous, Christians are very judgmental of other people who are not Christians. In discussions with others, their opinions are narrow-minded, based mainly on biblical principles. They discuss many subjects and base their answers and comments on only what's in the Bible, and they don't consider the opinion of others. And we know that the Bible has many errors and contradictions."

Mr. Cobra turned to the judge. "That's all I have at this time, Your Honor."

Judge El-Bib said, "Your witness, Mr. Devas."

Mr. Devas said, "Thank you, Your Honor. During my closing statement, I will address these horrible accusations of character flaws like intolerance, unforgiveness, arrogance, and pompousness that were just mentioned by Mr. Eagle. Mr. Eagle, first of all, what is your opinion of the Bible?"

Mr. Eagle answered, "I believe that it is a purely fictional book. For example, the story of the three guys in a fire who walked out unharmed! That's not possible."

"You may be interested to know that similar events have occurred in history. Polycarp (AD 69–155) was a Christian bishop of Smyrna. According to the *Martyrdom of Polycarp*, he died a martyr, bound and burned at the stake, then stabbed when the fire failed to consume his body. Now back to your character flaw criticisms. Isn't it true that many people in general are hypocrites?"

"Yes, I believe some are."

Mr. Devas said, "Jesus directed us to be bold and rational, but definitely not arrogant or bossy. If you saw or heard a Christian acting or speaking in an unwholesome manner, I apologize for him/her and all others. Some Christians, especially those who are young and new to the faith, get excited when sharing about Jesus with unbelievers."

Mr. Eagle replied, "Well, maybe, but let me ask you a question. Since you say Jesus was a nice guy, shouldn't these so-called young Christians follow the actions of Jesus?"

"Yes. As I just said, they are being bold and rational but definitely not arrogant or bossy. In another comment, you stated that 'hypocrisy (a pretense to be what one is not) is the worst character flaw a human can have.'"

Mr. Cobra called out, "Objection, Your Honor. Mr. Devas is acting like a witness."

Mr. Devas said, "Your witness asked me a question."

Judge El-Bib said, "Objection overruled. Ask a question, Mr. Devas."

Mr. Devas replied, "Yes, Your Honor." He turned to Mr. Eagle. "Is it possible that when Jesus, our Creator, speaks of human nature, He is referring to all humans, including Christians, as being profoundly fallen and deeply flawed?"

Mr. Eagle answered, "Yes, it's true. All humans are flawed. But my understanding is that Christians are to try to be perfect."

"You have it right. Christians should try to be perfect as Jesus is perfect. That is their goal, but there is no way—I repeat, there is no way for anyone on this good earth to be even close to perfect. And how do you define perfect in this secular world without a universal standard?"

"Okay! First, when Christians try to follow Jesus, they always fall short. Second, if Christians believe in Jesus, then they should follow him, with no excuses."

Mr. Devas said, "Christians try to follow Jesus but 'always' fall short. Really? I believe that all Christians don't fall short. Yes, Christians are asked to follow Jesus, who is perfection—the only true standard for human behavior, which is all in the Bible. And, yes, Christians fall short, as does everyone in the world. The Bible says in Romans 3:23 (NKJV), 'For all have sinned and fall short of the glory of God.' You also say that most Christians seem to be intolerant or uncompromising and judgmental, and that they act in an arrogant and demanding manner toward others. Christians are taught that arrogance like pride is a sin."

Mr. Cobra said, "I object. Mr. Devas is testifying."

Mr. Devas replied, "I am simply responding to Mr. Eagle's comment."

Judge El-Bib said, "Objection overruled. Please continue, Mr. Devas."

Mr. Devas continued. "Isn't it true that Christian doctrine conflicts with current secular thought? That it is the secular thought that is changing? If so, then Christians are wrongly judged for being intolerant when they are just being bold"—**he raised his voice**—"as

IS THE BIBLE NECESSARY?

Jesus directed them to be, and are just presenting truth, for the Bible never changes spiritual truth."

Mr. Eagle said, "The fact still remains that Christians will argue about most spiritual subjects."

"Really? Argue, or REASON and obey? Jesus commanded His apostles and all Christians, and this is very important as I read, in **Matthew 28:19–20 (NKJV)**, 'Go therefore and make disciples of all the nations, baptizing them in the name of the Father and of the Son and of the Holy Spirit, teaching them to observe all things that I have commanded you; and lo, I am with you always, even to the end of the age.' Jesus is God." There was a long pause. "So do Christians argue, or desire to reason and obey? Christ commanded all Christians to teach and to reason in love with all peoples concerning all that is in the Bible, as the verse that I just read says. Isn't that so, Mr. Eagle?"

Mr. Eagle replied, "I would have to say they argue mostly."

"You also said of Christians in general that most, when in church, will act like they are the pillar of the community. However, when in a secular environment, like at a party, many of them will display sinful behaviors. They were heard cursing and seen flirting too much. Isn't it true that your attention was so focused on Christians that you tended to look away from others? And by the way, how did you know who at the function were Christians?"

"We came to that conclusion by the conversations we had with each person."

"It's important to note that Christian critics who cry 'Intolerant!' have a distorted view of what tolerance really entails. True tolerance does not demand that one person accepts another's views as valid. Rather, it demands that we show respect toward others who don't share our values, beliefs, and practices. Let us be ashamed of any moment in which we disrespect, mock, or condemn any persons for their beliefs and lifestyle choices, *because we are all justified in having our opinions.* Christ won people's hearts and minds through his respectful treatment of each person. Shouldn't we follow Christ's example, especially since He is God?"

Mr. Cobra said, "Objection, Your Honor. There is no evidence that Jesus is God."

Judge El-Bib said, "Objection sustained. Be careful, Mr. Devas. The jury will disregard the last comment by Mr. Devas."

Mr. Devas replied, "Yes, sir. Sorry, Your Honor. That's all I have for this witness."

Judge El-Bib asked, "Mr. Cobra, do you have anything further?"

Mr. Cobra replied, "No, thank you, Your Honor. We rest our case at this time."

Judge El-Bib then said, "Very well then. Since Mr. Eagle is the last witness for Mr. Cobra, we will stop for the day."

The judge excused the jury to their hotel rooms and set a time of 10:00 a.m. tomorrow to reconvene the trial. At that time, Mr. Devas would begin introducing his witnesses.

CHAPTER 12

DR. LIOS
ARCHAEOLOGY

Everyone was in place at 10:00 a.m. The bailiff called for the jury to enter.

Judge El-Bib said, "Mr. Devas, please call your first witness."

Mr. Devas announced, "Your Honor, our first witness will discuss the truth or fiction of archaeology. I call Dr. Lios to the stand."

The bailiff swore in the witness.

Mr. Devas said, "Good morning, Dr. Lios."

Dr. Lios replied, "Good morning."

"What is your background and your qualifications to be a witness here today? Please explain in detail to the jury."

Dr. Lios answered, "I am sixty-five years old. I have been married to my lovely wife for forty-one years. We have a son, age forty, who has two children, and our daughter, age thirty-eight, also has two children. For forty years, since 1981, I have worked in the field of archaeology. I have a doctorate in geology and archaeology from the University of Northern California.

"Beginning at the time of the Industrial Revolution (1760–1840), geology started to develop. James Hutton (1726–1797), a Scottish farmer and naturalist, is known as the founder of modern geology, from which archaeology followed. I personally have supervised the excavation of more than 125 digs in or near the Middle East. Most are in the areas mentioned in the Bible.

"You may ask, when did archaeology begin? Modern archaeology started at the end of the nineteenth century (1880–1900). During these times, many sites were excavated, and artifacts were collected just for pleasure or treasure. But at the beginning of the twentieth century, people started to see archaeology as an answer to many of the world's historical questions, as well as the Bible's.

"We are fortunate to live in a time of history that is so very rich in archaeological discoveries. In the last seventy years, the number of digs has increased dramatically. This is a marked contrast from previous centuries, when there was little evidence for the Bible. To fully share with you the importance of all the archaeological explorations would take more time than this trial would allow, so I will mention some digs of importance.

"Digs have steadily increased through the nineteenth century and on into the twentieth century and now the twenty-first century, with literally thousands of excavations. Much of the work, or digs, has been in the areas mentioned in the Bible. There have been countless locations, names, and treasures indicated in the Bible that have been verified (proven) with archaeological digs. More than 25,000 sites showing some connection with the Old Testament period have been located. That's 25,000 sites, and not one of the archaeological findings have shown the Bible to be wrong. When a dig involved an area of the Bible, it verified in detail the description in the Bible for that location."

Mr. Devas asked, "Do you know any experts in the field of archaeology who can verify your testimony?"

"Yes, I do. Dr. W. F. Albright (1891–1971), director of the William F. Albright School of Archaeological Research in Jerusalem, was a leading biblical archaeologist, scholar, and author of more than eight hundred publications. In his writings, he stated, 'Discovery after discovery has established the accuracy of innumerable details, and has brought increased recognition to the value of the Bible as a source of history.'" Looking at the jury, Dr. Lios continued, "There

IS THE BIBLE NECESSARY?

can be no doubt that archaeology has confirmed a substantial historicity of Old Testament tradition and the Bible as a whole."

"Have archaeological digs discovered references to famous people in the Bible who are well-known to the general public?"

"Yes, there have been many such discoveries. Avraham Biran (1909–2008), who is best known for heading excavations at Tel Dan in northern Israel. He directed the Institute of Archaeology at Hebrew Union College in Jerusalem. His team of archaeologists, in early 1990 at Tel Dan, near the foot of Mount Hermon, found a remarkable inscription from the ninth century BC. See the map on the monitor. The inscription refers to both 'the House of David' and 'the King of Israel.' There can be no doubt King David was a real person.

Map showing Mount Hermon and Tel Dan

"My family traveled with me on some trips. We were blessed to travel to Israel and to be at the excavation site one day in 1990. Our son, who was age nine, and our daughter, who was age seven, were quite excited about the large excavation of dirt. I had to keep a close watch on the excavation project, and my wife and I were extra careful for the safety of the children. I learned the use of a Bible verse very quickly on that work vacation.

"Our children were playing in this large excavation, but I was nervous that they might get hurt. So at one point, I yelled at them very sternly. Then I remembered the Bible verse by the apostle Paul, Ephesians 6:4 (NKJV): 'And you fathers, do not provoke your children…but bring them up in the training and admonition of the Lord.' So I quickly got into the excavation and showed my children what was dangerous and why."

Mr. Devas said, "Thank you! That biblical policy is very important for children. Now another question, Dr. Lios. A well-known artifact is the Cyrus Cylinder. What can you tell us about it?"

"You may have heard of Cyrus the Great, who ruled the Persian Empire from 559 to 530 BC and who is best known for his capture of Babylon in 539 BC. In the eighth century BC (778–732), Isaiah predicted this defeat (Isaiah 45:1–3) and went on to say that Cyrus would 'set my exiles free' (Isaiah 45:13). That Cyrus released the Jewish exiles from Babylon to return to Jerusalem is not only documented in the Bible (2 Chronicles 36:22–23; Ezra 1:2–4), but it is also implied on the Cyrus Cylinder. It dates from the sixth century BC and was discovered in the ruins of Babylon in Mesopotamia (modern Iraq) in 1879 by Hormuzd Rassam, an Iraqi Assyrian archaeologist. This ancient record states, 'I [Cyrus] gathered all their former inhabitants and returned to them their habitations.' It is currently in the possession of the British Museum. Hormuzd Rassam also discovered clay tablets that contained the *Epic of Gilgamesh*, the world's oldest literature. Documents written on clay tablets from around 2300 BC demonstrate that the names of the people and places in the patriarchal age (biblical figures, i.e. fathers, especially Abraham, Isaac, and Jacob), their accounts are genuine."

"I have heard of the Hittites. Why are they important?"

IS THE BIBLE NECESSARY?

Dr. Lios replied, "Even though the Hittites are mentioned forty-seven times in the Bible, scholars doubted that they existed because no historical evidence of such people had been found. Then in 1876, Hugo Winckler, a German archaeologist and historian, uncovered the capital of the Hittite Empire and unearthed five temples and ten thousand clay tablets. They were deciphered, and they showed that the Hittites did really exist in the area described in the Bible, in modern-day Turkey.

"There are other important excavations:

1. Most of the major cities of the Bible have been identified. For example, Jericho, Jerusalem, and Nineveh.
2. In 1868, an inscribed stone was excavated at Dibon. The stone mentions Mesha, king of Moab, and his overthrow of Israel; King Omri; and the God of Israel (Yahweh).
3. Sumerian tablets that came from Uruk, in southern Mesopotamia, record the confusion of language, like we have in the biblical account of the Tower of Babel, a ziggurat that was first attested in the late third millennium BC (Genesis 11:1–9). (A ziggurat is a rectangular stepped tower, sometimes surmounted by a temple.)
4. In 1799, the Rosetta Stone was discovered. The Rosetta Stone is one of the most important objects in the British Museum, as it holds the key to understanding Egyptian hieroglyphs—a script made up of small pictures, which was used originally in ancient Egypt for religious texts."

Dr. Lios continued, "You see, ladies and gentlemen of the jury, archaeology does in fact prove many portions of the Bible."

Mr. Devas said, "That's all the questions I have for this witness at this time."

Judge El-Bib asked Mr. Cobra if he would like to cross-examine the witness.

Mr. Cobra replied, "Yes, thank you, Your Honor." He turned to the witness. "Good morning, Dr. Lios. According to Mr. Devas, the Bible is the only book that describes the truth about our eternal destiny and what it takes to obtain glorious eternity. But we know that there have been literally millions of books written on every subject. There are scientific journals, novels, textbooks, and history books, and we know that some of the books that are written as fact are not fact at all. Isn't it true that the Bible is simply just another book?"

Dr. Lios replied, "Remember, the argument is that the Bible is the Word of God because Jesus says it is. And further, the Bible is the Word of God because the Bible itself says it is, and any alternative leads to absurdity. It's this last part of the argument that closes the loopholes and provides the proof that the Bible really is what it claims to be, whereas counterfeit religious books fall short.

"If the Bible were not the Word of God, Christians would have no foundation for all the things we take for granted, such as laws of logic, uniformity of nature, and morality. The law of noncontradiction (a proposition and its opposite cannot both be true), for example, is based on the self-consistent nature of the biblical God. The Bible says in **2 Timothy 2:13 (NKJV)**, 'If we are faithless, He remains faithful; He cannot deny Himself.' The Bible itself tells us that all knowledge depends on God. **Proverbs 1:7 (NKJV)** says, '*The fear of the Lord is the beginning of knowledge, but fools despise wisdom and instruction.*' **Colossians 2:3 (NKJV)** says, 'The mystery of God, both of the Father and of Christ, in whom are hidden all the treasures of wisdom and knowledge.'

"Most other religious books do not make the claim that all knowledge is deposited in their god, and if they did, they would not be able to make good on the claim. Therefore, the argument will only work for the Bible."

Mr. Cobra said, "What was mentioned previously is all well and good if the Bible is true. However, how do we know for sure? I believe that what the Bible says is just a bunch of fables and stories that have been changed throughout the last four thousand years. What do you say, Dr. Lios?"

Dr. Lios replied, "It's not a book that arrived in complete form at one point in history. Although it is viewed as one book, it's actually a collection of sixty-six books written over a period of some 1,500 years by forty different authors. None of the books contradict each other. On the contrary, they complement one another. It is called God's Word even though God did not physically write it. Instead, God worked through everyday people, inspired by God the Holy Spirit, to record what Christians accept as the Bible.

"The Old Testament is primarily an accurate record of God's dealings with His chosen people—the Hebrews/Jews. The New Testament continues the record with first-century accounts of the life and ministry of Jesus and the struggles faced by new Christians in a hostile culture. Jesus taught to all who came to listen about **peace and love** by following Him. Here is just one example of how this can happen. Please allow me to tell you about a true event.

"In 2005, I was in Nigeria, Africa. Two tribes were feuding, to a point where some were dying in the fighting. A moderator was able to get the leaders of the two tribes to meet. They were given a Bible with their own translation. After a few weeks of studying on their own, some of the members from each tribe agreed to try a joint study. With guidance, they started Bible study together. After a couple of months, it became proof positive that the Bible itself does promote peace, and eventually, love. Those two tribes continue to have Bible study to this day, and the feuding has stopped.

"The Bible makes some very distinctive truth claims. It claims, for instance, that God exists. It also claims that He has chosen to communicate with us through His creation, our moral conscience, and the Bible. Jesus claimed to be God in the flesh and that the only way for human beings to be saved is through Him. **John 10:30 (NKJV)** says, 'I AND THE FATHER ARE ONE.' Moreover, the death and resurrection of Jesus are the keys to Christian theology. These claims in the Bible either correspond to reality, or they do not. Christians believe that they do correspond to reality, that what is described in the Bible is true. God really exists, Jesus is not a myth, and the resurrection really happened."

Mr. Cobra said, "The archaeological evidence of the Bible is scarce. In fact, it is nonexistent. After two hundred years of Christian archaeologists digging up the whole Middle East, they haven't found any proof of the exodus of the Jews from Egypt, Hebrew slaves, or the ten plagues. NONE! And this from a nation of people who wrote

EVERYTHING down in stone! And Sinai has no proof of any large group of people traveling through it EVER! All of what I have said is true, of course. Is it not?"

Dr. Lios replied, "We find the Exodus mentioned *as a* real historical *event* throughout the Old Testament, including the books of Psalms, Joshua, Judges, 1 and 2 Samuel, 1 and 2 Kings, and in the Prophets. We should note that the Bible is not a single-source document. There are forty authors. It has multiple sources, all of which maintain the authenticity of the Exodus tradition. Historians recognize that the likelihood of the authenticity of an event increases as independent sources that verify it are discovered. With this overwhelming evidence within the Bible regarding the Egyptian sojourn, exodus, and wilderness episodes, evidence coming from a variety of types of literature and used in a host of different ways, it is methodologically inadvisable, at best, to treat the Bible as a single witness to history, requiring corroboration before the Egypt-Sinai reports can be taken as authentic. Simply put, there is enough evidence contained in the Bible to make the account true.

"Moses is mentioned by many independent Bible authors, as are the Hebrews who were slaves in Egypt, and also the route detailed in the Bible where they escaped Egypt. It is likely such a man as Moses existed. If Jesus is God and He mentioned Moses dozens of times, Moses must be a real person. And this group of people called Israelites lived in Egypt, and these people left Egypt via the route detailed in the Bible. 'Many people today treat the Bible as being guilty until proven innocent,' said James Hoffmeier, an American Old Testament scholar, 'which doesn't seem fair, as who's around to prove it that lived back then?' I stand firmly in the camp that God can do what He says He's going to do, whether large or small. When I read of the Bible's miracles—from the miraculous parting of the Red Sea to the miraculous resurrection of Jesus—do I say 'I'm not believing it until I see definitive proof'? Rather, I say, 'Wow! Amazing!'

"Follow these truths: Jesus lived, Jesus is God, God cannot lie, and the Bible is true. Jesus mentioned Moses's name twenty-one times in the Bible. Thus, Moses is a real person who led the Exodus. Therefore, detailed archaeological information is not necessary for evidence about every step of the Exodus. Remember that most of the world's history is presented to us by a written account with no physical evidence."

Mr. Cobra said, "The first evidence correlating to the biblical story doesn't appear in Canaan archaeology until around one hundred years before the Babylonian captivity (around 600 BC). This lack of evidence includes persons such as David and Solomon, who should be recorded in other nations and historical records and who supposedly lived relatively close to those who wrote the Bible in the Babylonian captivity, around 500 BC."

Dr. Lios replied, "As I mentioned earlier, an excavation by Avraham Biram and his team of archaeologists in early 1990 at Tel Dan, near the foot of Mount Hermon, found a remarkable inscription from the ninth century BC. The inscription refers to both 'the House of David' and 'the King of Israel.' And further, King David lived in the era of 1000 BC, not 500 BC."

"No evidence of the events described in the book of Genesis has ever been found. No city walls have been found at Jericho from the appropriate era that could have been toppled by Joshua or otherwise. The stone palace uncovered at the foot of the Temple Mount in Jerusalem could attest that King David had been there, or it might belong to another era entirely, depending who you ask."

"As to their evidence, Dr. Bryant Wood (1936–), a biblical archaeologist, director of the Associates for Biblical Research, and one of the leading experts on the archaeology of Jericho, recently pointed out that John Garstang (1930–1936) and Kathleen Kenyon (1952–1958) both dug at Jericho for six seasons, and a German excavation directed by Ernst Sellin and Carl Watzinger dug for three seasons. All found abundant solid evidence of the city's destruction by fire in a layer related to the biblical date of 1400 BC."

Mr. Cobra turned to the judge. "I have nothing further at this time."

Judge El-Bib called for a lunch break.

*****

NOTE: Millar Burrows (1889–1980) was an American *biblical scholar*, a leading authority on the Dead Sea Scrolls, and professor emeritus at Yale Divinity School. Burrows was director of the American School of Oriental Research in Jerusalem (now the William F. Albright School of Archaeological Research), and he stated, "Archaeological work has unquestionably strengthened confidence in the reliability of the scriptural record… This is a real contribution and not to be minimized."

CHAPTER 13

Dr. Rubin
Bible Translations

Everyone was in place at 2:00 p.m. The bailiff called for the jury to enter.

Judge El-Bib said, "Mr. Devas, please call your next witness."

Mr. Devas said, "I call Dr. Rubin, our second witness, to the stand."

The bailiff swore in the witness.

Mr. Devas greeted the witness. "Good morning, Dr. Rubin."

Dr. Rubin replied, "Good morning."

"Please tell us a little bit about yourself, including your line of work, in detail."

Dr. Rubin answered, "I am seventy-three years old and have a beautiful wife and three adult children. I have a doctorate in Bible history, and for forty-three years, since 1977, I have worked in the field of Bible translations. In that period, my company, named Be Exact, has reviewed numerous new versions of the Bible, most of which have been published, and all are flawless. They are flawless. Be Exact, a partnership started in 1985 has thirty employees, twenty of whom have doctorates in different fields of science and theology."

"Dr. Rubin, why is it you have chosen this profession?"

"As I was growing up, I was surrounded by many Christian adults, including my parents, who instilled in me a passion and a love for reading and studying the Bible. Because of that, it has become a strong desire of mine for all people to know who Jesus is and what He tells us in the Bible.

"Being a translator is more than just copying words from another language. Each language requires detailed study in Hebrew and Greek, and many important documents to make sure that the words in the new translation are exactly as they are in our modern Bibles. That means the new translation must be and will be inerrant. We have a big advantage over the translators of, say, five hundred or one thousand years ago. The authors used scribes or secretaries to write down what was dictated, or they copied existing pages. Years ago, when a Bible was to be copied, the scribes were required to follow a very detailed set of rules for each word, verse, and even a period or comma. I will detail the Talmudists' intricate system for transcribing a little later."

Mr. Devas turned to the judge. "Your Honor, I have no more questions for this witness at this time."

Judge El-Bib said, "Mr. Cobra, would you care to cross-examine this witness?"

Mr. Cobra replied, "Thank you, Your Honor. Yes, I have a few questions." He turned to the witness. "Is it true, Dr. Rubin, that you have only been working on Bible translations published since 1977? And isn't it also true that there were hundreds of Bible translations written by various people before 1977?"

Dr. Rubin answered, "Yes, that's true. However, there have been—"

Mr. Cobra interrupted. "Excuse me, Dr. Rubin. A yes or no answer will be sufficient."

Mr. Devas said, "I object, Your Honor. Dr. Rubin should be allowed to explain the details of his work."

Judge El-Bib said, "The objection is sustained."

Mr. Devas replied, "Thank you, Your Honor."

Judge El-Bib turned to the witness. "Dr. Rubin, please continue with your comment."

Dr. Rubin said, "There have been hundreds of Bible translations written. The whole Bible was canonized in the Council of

IS THE BIBLE NECESSARY?

Nicaea AD 325, which means the Bible was accepted as true and complete at that time. Also, I must note that our organization has reviewed all or most of these translations. We have found 98 percent of the translations from before 1974 to be inerrant. We have a list of all the Bibles that have been written and a copy of most. There are only about fifteen to twenty Bible versions used by most people in the world today.

"Please understand, Mr. Cobra. Again I say that 98 percent of the Bibles that have been printed in the last few hundred years have been reviewed and are, as I said before, all inerrant, having been compared to, and I repeat, reliable manuscripts, including the very valuable Dead Sea Scrolls, which were found in Qumran, east of Jerusalem, in 1947; the Septuagint, written around 300 BC; the Masoretic Text, copied, edited, and distributed by a group of Jews known as the Masoretes between the seventh and tenth centuries AD; and other very old manuscripts. By the way, a copy of all versions of the Bible are in museums around the world."

Mr. Cobra replied, "Thank you, Dr. Rubin. Your Honor, I have no further questions for this witness at this time."

Judge El-Bib asked, "Mr. Devas, do you wish to recross-examine?"

Mr. Devas replied, "Yes. Thank you, Your Honor. Dr. Rubin, how can you assure the jury that each of your Bible reviews are accurate?"

Dr. Rubin answered, "We have a photostatic translation camera that takes photos and reviews the new languages for accuracy. The camera was designed by our partners at our company, Be Exact. We place pages from two translations on the table. One is an English version that has been scrutinized for inerrancy, and we compare it to a copy of the new language for exact accuracy using organized assistance substantiating translation (OAST).

"One of our language specialists reviews each page for accuracy. After checking all pages, we have an entire Bible in a new language that is ready for printing and placed in missionaries' computer tablets. The missionaries also carry a mini printer. When a missionary goes to a village, a portion or all of the new Bible can be printed and given to the leaders (mayors) and the folks who live there." Looking at the jury, Dr. Rubin stated, "It is hard to explain how excited the village or town folks are when they receive a Bible in their language. Also, audios in some languages are available."

Mr. Devas said, "Please tell us more about the safekeeping of biblical records."

"The preservation of the Bible has been carefully guarded over the centuries. As much as handwritten copies were cherished, slight errors may have been made along the way, yet the possibility is minuscule. See 'The Talmudists,' which I will show on the screen.

"In 1844, Constantin Tischendorf first discovered the Codex Sinaiticus, an ancient copy of the Bible that was compiled in the fourth century AD. A codex is a book made from animal skin, called vellum. This method of bookmaking was used from the fourth to the fifteenth century. In 1844, forty-three leaves of a fourth-century biblical codex (a collection of single pages bound together along one side) were discovered in a monastery at the foot of Mount Sinai. When Constantin arrived at the monastery, he found the priests burning the pages of the manuscript to keep warm!

"This was not, however, the only codex on the Holy Scriptures that had been copied. After the fifteenth century, the Vatican brought forth their Codex Vaticanus, which has been dated, relating to writings of former times, back to the fourth century. This written copy was previously unknown to the world and yet is still well intact.

"God has preserved throughout the ages His Word, which we now can hold in our own hands and respond to with our hearts. Copies of each codex are in the computers in your rooms. Also in your computer is the list of steps required for a Talmudist to follow while copying a book of the Scripture. It's on the monitor now."

> The Talmudists (AD 100–500)
>
> During this period, a great deal of time was spent in cataloging Hebrew civil and canonical law. The Talmudists had quite an intricate system for transcribing synagogue scrolls.

IS THE BIBLE NECESSARY?

Samuel Davidson (1806–1898) describes some of the disciplines of the Talmudists in regard to the scriptures. These extensive regulations include directions down to the most minute detail. Using the numbering incorporated by Geisler and Nix, these directions are as follows:

(1) A synagogue roll must be written on the skins of clean animals and (2) must be prepared by a Jew for the particular use of the synagogue by the priests. (3) These must be fastened together with strings taken from clean animals. (4) Every skin must contain a certain number of columns, equal throughout the entire codex. (5) The length of each column must not extend over less than forty-eight or more than sixty lines, and the breadth must consist of thirty letters. (6) The whole copy must first be lined, and if three words be written without a line, it is worthless. (7) The ink should be black, neither red nor green nor any other color, and must be prepared according to a definite recipe. (8) An authentic copy must be the exemplar, from which the transcriber ought not in the least deviate. (9) No word or letter, not even a yod (period), must be written from memory, with the scribe not having looked at the codex before him. (10) Between every consonant, the space of a hair or thread must intervene; (11) between every new parashah, or section, the breadth of nine consonants; and (12) between every book, three lines. (13) The fifth book of Moses must terminate exactly with a line, but the rest need not do so. (14) Besides this, the copyist must sit in full Jewish dress, (15) wash his whole body, (16) not begin to write the name of God with a pen newly dipped in ink,

and (17) should a king address him while writing that name, he must take no notice of him.

Dr. Rubin continued, "History tells us that if these regulations were not observed, the scrolls were condemned to be buried in the ground or burned, or they were banished to the schools, to be used for reading only."

Mr. Devas said, "Dr. Rubin, please review for us if there have been recent discoveries concerning the Bible that help to verify today's Bible."

Dr. Rubin replied, "The more recent discoveries of the Dead Sea Scrolls, which were written 150 to 200 years before Christ, match with our own King James Version of the Bible and others. The Isaiah Scroll from Qumran, near the Dead Sea, east of Jerusalem, was the most complete scroll found.

"As we know, papyrus is the first known material used in writing. It was made from a plant and used as paper until about the fourth century BC. Thousands of fragments of papyrus scrolls were found near Qumran, and most have been compiled and translated. And at each completion, none have failed to agree with our own King James Version of the Bible.

"Through the work of archaeologists, there has been confirmation after confirmation of the validity of God's Word. Many times, the critics would say that there was no way a certain thing could have happened or a person could have been alive to be a part of what Scripture declares. But archaeological discoveries are proving daily over and over again that the Bible is in fact totally accurate and all that it claims. We can read the Bible with confidence that it is in fact inspired by GOD THE HOLY SPIRIT and is the unfailing Word of God."

Mr. Devas turned to the judge. "Your Honor, this is all we have at this time for this witness. However, we would like the chance to call him back at a future time."

Judge El-Bib asked Mr. Cobra if he had any further questions for the witness.

IS THE BIBLE NECESSARY?

Mr. Cobra answered, "Yes, Your Honor." He then rose from his chair in a very dignified manner and thanked the judge. Judge El-Bib nodded. Mr. Cobra approached Dr. Rubin, who was still in the witness stand, and said, "You state that you have a photostatic translation camera. We know for a fact that there are nearly one million words in the Bible. How can your machine have an inerrant accuracy for that many words? From all common sense, that just seems to be impossible. Dr. Rubin, what do you have to say?"

Dr. Rubin replied, "As you know, Mr. Cobra, and I'm sure the jury knows, electronic technology has skyrocketed in the last seventy years or so, and especially since the year 2000. Examples of this technology include the flash drive, the iPad, video streaming, smartphones, etc. With this in mind, Mr. Cobra, one can only be amazed and astonished at the kind of computer power each of us holds at our fingertips. Never mind that we use computers for frivolous matters. Imagine what we might hold in our hands twenty years from now. Therefore, it's easy to understand how our photostatic translation camera has an inherent accuracy to do incredible work unheard of just a few years ago. The Bible is flawless."

Dr. Rubin finished his testimony with the following statement: "It is well-known that many translator groups are translating the Bible without any errors, in record numbers, in record time, and also in many languages. It would be a disaster if the Bible was removed from society."

Judge El-Bib asked, "Any further questions, Mr. Cobra?"

Mr. Cobra replied, "No, Your Honor."

Judge El-Bib turned to the other lawyer. "Mr. Devas?"

Mr. Devas said, "No, thank you, Your Honor. I thank Dr. Rubin for his splendid testimony."

Judge El-Bib called for the end of the fourth day.

CHAPTER 14

THE JOURNALIST PERSPECTIVE

Jon Martin, the Pastor from Lagoa, Portugal, was speaking to a group of Christians in a hall nearby. "The anticipation is growing as the crowds grow here in Jerusalem, and the media increases their daily coverage. The case against the Bible continues to take the top spot in the news. Outside the court building, large crowds have gathered to support or protest both sides of the court case. In addition, around the world, there are crowds at churches and government centers. The crowds, numbering in the thousands, are waiting patiently for the verdict of the trial of the century.

"Multiple media organizations are also present here and around the world, wherever the crowds have formed. The defense team for the Bible in this trial must use caution when answering questions posed by the media, to assure that information given either in verbal or written form is not misinterpreted. Wherever misinformation is discovered, the defense team, guided by the Holy Spirit, must counter it with the facts of the case.

"The Bible consists of sixty-six separate books, which God inspired forty authors to write without error. The individual books were written over the course of 1,500 years, in many locations and for different people groups. God the Holy Spirit inspired prophets—for example, Moses and Apostles Paul and Peter—to write about God's relationship with His people and the world. For example, **2 Peter 1:20–21 (NKJV)** says, 'Knowing this first, that no prophecy

IS THE BIBLE NECESSARY?

of Scripture is of any private interpretation, for prophecy never came by the will of man, but holy men of God spoke as they were moved by the Holy Spirit.' Therefore, the subjects in all sixty-six books in the Bible interconnect as a compilation of human history, wisdom literature, prophecy, and God's plan for the world.

"The Bible has been the most scrutinized book in history, critiqued and analyzed by hundreds of people and organizations throughout history. In spite of the relentless challenges, no errors in doctrine have been found in it. To repeat, zero errors have been found in the Bible. The Dead Sea Scrolls, discovered in caves in Israel over the last seventy-five years, attest to this fact. You can research the findings yourself, along with other ancient manuscripts like the Codex Vaticanus, the Codex Sinaiticus, and the Masoretic Text. The defense team believes that the information that will come out in this trial will give strong evidence and proof that the Bible is, without a doubt, necessary and beneficial for all mankind."

CHAPTER 15

DR. SANDBERG THE BIBLE IS PERFECTION

Everyone was in place at 10:00 a.m. The bailiff called for the jury to enter.

Judge El-Bib said, "Mr. Devas, please call your next witness."

Mr. Devas replied, "Your Honor, our third witness will be Dr. Sandberg."

The bailiff swore in the witness.

Mr. Devas said, "Dr. Sandberg, please tell the jury what qualifies you to be an expert witness for this trial."

Dr. Sandberg replied, "I have doctorates from Grace University in Bible history and theology. I've enjoyed my profession for twenty-five years and have taught various religious classes at Grace University. After I received my doctorates, I took classes in Hebrew and Greek to better understand the original writings of the Bible."

"Thank you. What is the difference in meaning of *infallible*, *perfect*, and *inerrant*?"

"The dictionary definitions are as follows: *Infallible* means 'incapable of error in defining doctrines.' *Inerrant* means 'free from error.' *Perfect* means 'flawless.' Therefore, the Bible is exact, and it is perfect in context and content. The Bible is without error throughout every historical event."

IS THE BIBLE NECESSARY?

"Doesn't the Bible change throughout history?"

Dr. Sandberg answered, "It is important to remember that the biblical manuscripts we have today are 99 percent in agreement with one another. A previous witness covered this area completely. Yes, there are some minor differences, but all the biblical texts are identical in subject matter from one manuscript (version) to another. Most of the differences are in punctuation, word endings, minor grammatical issues, word order, etc.—issues easily explainable as scribal mistakes or changes in spelling rules. No important theological subject matter is thrown into doubt. Biblical manuscripts from the fifteenth century agree completely with manuscripts from the third century and the Dead Sea Scrolls. We can have absolute confidence that the Bible we have today is identical to all historical manuscripts. It's the same as what the apostles and prophets wrote 2,000 to 4,500 years ago.

"Concerning the Bible, Jesus himself stated in John 10:35, 'And the Scripture cannot be broken,' thus testifying to the authority of the Bible. **Matthew 5:18 (NKJV)** says, 'For assuredly, I say to you, till heaven and earth pass away, one jot or one tittle will by no means pass from the law till all is fulfilled.'

"I would like to address a common criticism concerning contradictions in the Bible. Allow me to draw an example of a supposed contradiction in a secular event. There is a hit-and-run car accident. One witness says that the car that took off was black, and another witness says the car was dark gray. However, the accident is the primary concern, and the color of the car does not change that.

"Jesus warns against misleading any of His little ones, by mouth or written word, in **Matthew 18:5–6 (NKJV)**. He says, 'Whoever receives one little child like this in My name receives Me. Whoever causes one of these little ones who believe in Me to sin, it would be better for him if a millstone were hung around his neck, and he were drowned in the depth of the sea.' Jesus's heartbeat is evident throughout Scripture. We must be on guard, mainly through prayer, not to allow any errors concerning His Word, because His Word is His heart and will."

Mr. Devas asked, "Why is it important to believe in biblical inerrancy?"

Dr. Sandberg replied, "If one person altered the Bible, then why not others? Do you agree that would violate the integrity or truth for any book? We live in a time when too many people tend to shrug when confronted with an error of any kind. Instead of asking, like Pilate, 'What is truth?' postmodern man says 'Nothing is truth' or perhaps 'There is truth, but we cannot know it.' We've grown accustomed to being lied to (like with fake news), and many people seem comfortable with the false notion that the Bible, too, contains errors. Simply put, the Bible cannot have ANY errors in doctrine. It's all or nothing at all."

"Tell us about Noah's flood and the dispersion."

"Many people believe that there are **seven parts** for the Gospel of Jesus Christ. **First** would be the **creation**, when Jesus created everything six thousand years ago. **Second** would be the **fall and sin** by Adam and Eve. **Third**, the event that follows next would be Noah's flood and the dispersion of the people from Babel. It says in **Genesis 11:7–8 (NKJV)**, 'Come, let Us go down and there confuse their language, that they may not understand one another's speech. So the Lord scattered them abroad from there over the face of all the earth, and they ceased building the city.'

"Due to the dispersion of people all over the world, evidence of the flood has been found by archaeologists excavating around the world, with an extensive amount found in the Middle East. They found drawings carved in cave walls, clay tablets with depictions of the flood, and the like where the people settled after the dispersion from Babel, which shows us evidence/proof of the flood of Genesis 11:9. Archaeology has proved to us that many different languages existed about 4,500 years ago, and it has given us evidence that the worldwide flood actually happened. Archaeologists have found fossils of sea creatures in rock layers that cover all the continents. For example, in the US, in the state of Arizona, most of the rock layers in the walls of the Grand Canyon, which is more than a mile above sea level, contain marine fossils.

IS THE BIBLE NECESSARY?

"The flood and the dispersion evidence show again that the Bible is true. Jesus Christ Himself said to His followers in Mark 1:15, 'Believe the Gospel.' What gospel was He talking about? Besides Christ's birth, death, resurrection/ascension, and future return to earth, Christ was telling us that creation, the fall, and the flood are part of the gospel, which total the seven parts of it as I mentioned before."

Mr. Devas asked, "Do other religions have holy books? If so, what are their main claims?"

Dr. Sandberg replied, "Mr. Patrick Zukeran, Executive Director of Evidence and Answers, a research and teaching ministry specializing in Christian apologetics, stated that there are many books today that claim to be the Word of God. The Koran, the Islam holy book, claims to be the Word of God. The Book of Mormon claims to be the Word of God. The Hindus believe the Bhagavad Gita is the source of eternal truth. Karl Marx, with an atheistic worldview, claimed that his writing, *The Communist Manifesto*, was the ultimate truth."

"Dr. Sandberg, in your professional opinion, what do you consider to be the Bible's authority (the power to influence) in the world? And how do we know the Bible is the Word of God?"

"What is the authority of the Bible? It is the Word of God, although we can't prove everything. But there is some proof that the Bible is true and inerrant—and much evidence. In the history of man, there has not been a book that has rocked the world as the Bible has. The impact it has made is phenomenal. Some hail the Bible as the Word of God. Others criticize and condemn it. With the Bible facing such great opposition today, as we see in this trial, again we ask, how do we know the Bible is the true Word of God?

"There is overwhelming support from history that the Bible is 100 percent accurate. The idea that the Bible might contain errors is a relatively new belief. Harold Lindsell, who was one of the founding members of Fuller Theological Seminary, stated, 'Apart from a few exceptions, the church through the ages has consistently believed that the entire Bible is the inerrant or infallible Word of God' (*The Battle for the Bible*, Zondervan, 1978, 42–43). And when you hear the utterances of the prophets spoken as it were personally, you must not suppose that they are spoken by the inspired men themselves but by the divine Word who moves them (*First Apology*, 36 written by Justin Martyr) (AD 100–165).

"Jesus warns His disciples about the attitude the world will have toward those who follow Him. He says in **John 15:17–19 (NKJV)**, 'These things I command you, that you love one another. If the world hates you, you know that it hated Me before it hated you. If you were of the world, the world would love its own. Yet because you are not of the world, but I chose you out of the world, therefore the world hates you.' With that in mind, C. S. Lewis, in his book *Mere Christianity*, stated that Jesus was either a liar and a lunatic or Lord of all creation. In the Bible, the Lord Jesus left nothing in between to consider.

"The world is and always has been in rebellion against Him. Worldly people who do not believe the Bible seek to discredit our faith. In light of the times we live in, with deadly riots, looting, anarchy, senseless destruction of cities, and a world virus killing millions, it is important that Christians know not only what they believe, but also why they believe what they believe. That's why all people should know what the Bible says about life."

Mr. Devas said, "Thank you, Dr. Sandberg. Your Honor, this is all we have for this witness."

Judge El-Bib said, "Your witness, Mr. Cobra."

Mr. Cobra replied, "Thank you, Your Honor. Dr. Sandberg, do you believe all that is in the Bible?"

Dr. Sandberg answered, "Yes, the Bible is the most reliable and truthful book ever written. It not only has answers concerning Christianity, but it verifies many aspects of science, including guidance for sanitation and diet. The Bible is also a history book with guiding principles for living a good life that has been used by many countries, including the United States, for centuries prior to any books being written exclusively for schools. It's a fact: there is no book that has been scrutinized, criticized, and attacked more than the Bible. Many intelligent scholars have written books that attempt to discredit the authority of the Bible. One of Satan's goals is to tempt man to doubt the Word of God and thus doubt Jesus."

"In my opinion, Jesus was just a man, and his opinion is just that—an opinion. If I am correct, why should his statements hold any more weight than mine?"

"Consider your parents, teachers, and bosses who helped you in your youth. You respected many of them, I'm sure. How much more should we respect wise counsel from the God-man, Jesus?"

"According to what I've read and what I've heard, Jesus had a very large following. It seems to me all the notoriety and power went to his head, and the only thing it got him was crucifixion. But his apostles, in order to save face, continued and perpetuated Jesus's story, which is full of lies. And this is all understandable. Do you agree that is probably what happened?"

Dr. Sandberg replied, "My short answer is NO. But after you study Christianity and the Bible, you will find that all the talk about the Bible and Christianity is true, and you will discover that Jesus is not a liar and a lunatic. He is the Lord of all creation, as stated by C. S. Lewis in his book *Mere Christianity*. Further, I believe with all my heart that after your study, you will determine that Christianity is the only true religion and that the Bible is, in fact, exact.

"Ladies and gentlemen of the jury, as has been mentioned to you before, you have numerous resources on your computer from Mr. Cobra, Mr. Devas, and me. By studying, I believe you will come to the conclusion that the Bible is true and that all charges being brought in this trial are baseless."

Mr. Cobra asked, "Why on earth would a god, if there is one, lower himself or herself to be a mere human? And to top it off by saying that he/she is the *creator, god, and savior*? Really? Answer me. Why does this happen?"

Dr. Sandberg replied, "Those are interesting questions that will take some time to answer, but I will try to be brief. My comments are made with the consideration that the Bible is inerrant. In answering your first question, God the Father sent His Son Jesus (God the Son) into the world to 'become flesh,' as the Bible puts it, in order to take humanity into Himself. He then died a death of sacrificial atonement—the innocent for the guilty. It's a central Christian doctrine, incarnation, that God became flesh. This is key in understanding

God's purpose for your life. God has numbered your days and will fulfill every purpose He has for you.

"To answer your second question, is Jesus *Creator, God, and Savior?* It all begins in Genesis, where God, Jesus, makes the statement in **Genesis 1:26–27 (NKJV)**: 'Let Us make man in Our image, according to Our likeness; let them have dominion over the fish of the sea, over the birds of the air, and over the cattle, over all the earth and over every creeping thing that creeps on the earth. So God created man in His own image; in the image of God He created him; male and female He created them.' You see, Jesus is stating that He is the Creator and that He is God the Son, the second person in the Trinity.

"John the Apostle makes a similar statement in his gospel. He says in **John 1:3 (NKJV)**, 'All things were made through Him, and without Him nothing was made that was made.' And *Jesus himself said* in John 5:24 (NKJV), 'Most assuredly, I say to you, he who hears My word and believes in Him who sent Me has everlasting life, and shall not come into judgment, but has passed from death into life.' *So there it is. Jesus is Creator, God, and Savior*, and the Bible is His love letter to each of us personally. Other witnesses have given you sufficient evidence indicating that the Bible is perfect. So when you put these three verses together with the Bible, they indicate without a doubt that Jesus is the Creator, God, and Savior.

"Now for a brief explanation concerning Genesis 1:26, which states, 'Let Us make man.' This verse refers to what is called the Trinity, which is comprised of God the Father, Jesus (God the Son), and God the Holy Spirit. There are not three Gods but three persons in one God. I'll give you a couple of examples. Consider the sun, if you will. It has three functions, but you only see one. It gives heat, gives light, and has gravity. Also consider a person like me, comprised of body, mind, and spirit. Each is separate, but I need all three to be me. The Trinity may very well be the biggest mystery in Christianity and may be impossible to explain. Jesus said in John 10:30, 'I and My Father are one.' In addition, the Bible states in the book of Colossians 2:9 (NKJV), 'For in Christ all the fullness of the Deity lives in bodily form.'"

IS THE BIBLE NECESSARY?

Mr. Cobra interrupted. "Dr. Sandberg, your answer is based on the premise that the Bible is inerrant. I don't believe that the Bible is inerrant, and I don't believe that members of the jury do. Please explain."

Dr. Sandberg replied, "Well, that's very sad to hear. As I said before, I strongly urge you to study the Bible, chapter by chapter, and you will determine for yourself that it is inerrant. Once you do, you will realize that all I have said is true because the entire Bible is based on truth."

"The vast majority of the world is not Christian, so what happens to the majority of people after they die? Remember, much of the world's populace holds different opinions concerning the afterlife."

"The human opinion does not matter. We can only be assured of what God says. His actual words are in the Holy Bible. So!

1. If Christianity is true, true believers are guaranteed the afterlife with Jesus. Those who don't believe that Jesus is God have a problem.
2. Also, Jesus said in **Matthew 7:13 (NKJV)**, 'Enter by the narrow gate; for wide is the gate and broad is the way that leads to destruction, and there are many who go in by it.'
3. For those who have never heard about Jesus, He has said in His book, the Bible, in **Ecclesiastes 3:11 (NKJV)**, 'He has made everything beautiful in its time. Also He has put eternity in their hearts, except that no one can find out the work that God does from beginning to end.'
4. So this mystery of God (Jesus) is in everyone's heart.
5. If Christianity is false, I WILL still be okay in the afterlife if I am a good person. That follows for all the other people in the world.
6. However, only Jesus knows the heart of each of us, and thus, only He will decide where each of us will go in the afterlife AFTER WE DIE.

"But is it worth the gamble of your life for all eternity to not believe in Jesus and His book, the Bible? At the very least, find out what Jesus teaches."

There was a long pause as Mr. Cobra stayed silent.

Judge El-Bib asked, "Do you have further questions, Mr. Cobra?"

Mr. Cobra answered, "Yes, Your Honor! May I have a five-minute break to consult with my counsel?"

Judge El-Bib replied, "We will break for five minutes." He pounded the gavel lightly.

When the court proceedings reconvened, Mr. Cobra said to the witness, "You have talked a lot about the Bible being inerrant. If Noah's flood is true, millions of people died, including children. It seems to me that the Christian God is ruthless, isn't He?"

Dr. Sandberg answered, "No! We need to realize that the flood was part of preparing the world for Jesus and human salvation. This does not negate the emotional impact of drowning children, but it does provide perspective. The God of the flood is the same God who came in human form, Jesus, to be brutalized, humiliated, and murdered"—he raised his voice—"as a sacrifice for us all. That same God, Jesus, provided a way for all people to be redeemed and rescued from an eternal hell, by rising from the dead. Including all those at the time of Noah. And as I said earlier, for those who have never heard about Jesus, He has said in His book, the Bible, in **Ecclesiastes 3:11 (NKJV)**, 'He has made everything beautiful in its time. Also He has put eternity in their hearts, except that no one can find out the work that God does from beginning to end.' So this mystery of God (Jesus), **eternity**, is in everyone's heart."

Mr. Cobra shook his head and said, "I have nothing further at this time."

Judge El-Bib turned to the other lawyer. "Mr. Devas?"

Mr. Devas replied, "No, thank you, Your Honor, and thank you, Dr. Sandberg, for your splendid testimony."

Judge El-Bib called for a lunch break.

CHAPTER 16

DR. RUBIN (CONTINUED)

It was afternoon, and the judge asked Mr. Devas to call his next witness.

Mr. Devas said, "At this time, I would like to recall Dr. Rubin."

The bailiff reminded Dr. Rubin that he was still under oath.

Mr. Devas said to him, "Please discuss the New Testament compared with other works of antiquity."

Dr. Rubin answered, "The New Testament documents vividly picture the comparison between the New Testament and ancient historical writings. Perhaps we can appreciate how wealthy the New Testament is if it can be affirmed that the Bible is true and genuine. Let's compare the Bible with the textual material for other ancient historical works. A chart showing these numbers is on the monitor and in your computers.

"For Caesar's *Gallic War* (composed between 58 and 50 BC), there are several existing manuscripts (MSS), but only nine or ten are good. The oldest is some nine hundred years later than Caesar's day. Of the twenty books of *Histories* by Tacitus (AD 100), only four and a half survive. Of the sixteen books of his *Annals*, ten survive in full and two in part. The text of these existing portions of his two great historical works depends entirely on two MSS, one of the ninth century and one of the eleventh. Other scholars also commented that there is no ancient literature in the world that enjoys such a wealth of good textual evidence as the New Testament.

"When comparing the original manuscripts of the New Testament with those of ancient secular history, the number of New Testament manuscripts are numerous. Note that the number of New Testament copies far exceed all the other authors combined, and the earliest copy is very close to the actual event."

Number of Manuscripts Compared to Other Historical Writings

Author	Date written	Earliest discovered copy	Time span	Number of copies
Caesar	58–50 BC	AD 900	1,000 years	10
Plato	427–347 BC	AD 900	1,200 years	7
Aristotle	384–322 BC	AD 1100	1,400 years	49
Tacitus	AD 100	AD 1100	1,000 years	20
Pliny the Younger	AD 61–112	AD 850	750 years	7
Suetonius	AD 75–160	AD 950	800 years	8
Sophocles	AD 496–406	AD 1000	1,400 years	193
Homer	900 BC	400 BC	500 years	643
New Testament	AD 48–110	AD 125	15–90 years	24,633

Dr. Rubin continued, "According to Harold Greenlee, Professor of New Testament Greek at Asbury Seminary, and Dr. Ralph Wilson, Director of Joyful Heart Renewal Ministries, scholars accept as generally trustworthy the writings of the ancient classics, even though the earliest manuscripts (MSS) were written long after the original writings and the number of existing MSS is, in many instances, so small. Therefore, it is clear that the reliability of the text of the New Testament is likewise assured.

"I realize that when I talk about textual criticism, some will confuse it with higher criticism, which sometimes seems like a synonym for modern unbelief. They are completely different. Textual criticism is the fancy name for the discipline of determining as closely as possible which was the original text of a New Testament gospel or epistle as it came from the pen of its divinely inspired author or his secretary. Higher **criticism** is the study of biblical writings to determine their literary history and the purpose and meaning of the authors. Sometimes people choke on the word *criticism*. It doesn't mean 'to judge.' It is a technical term for 'the scientific investigation of literary documents (as in the Bible) in regard to such matters as origin, text, composition, or history.'"

Mr. Devas said, "That is all I have for now, Your Honor."

Judge El-Bib asked, "Mr. Cobra, do you have further questions for this witness?"

Mr. Cobra replied, "No, Your Honor, not at this time."

Judge El-Bib called for the end of the fifth day and indicated that court would resume tomorrow at 10:00 a.m.

Chapter 17

Dr. Lamb Apologetics

Everyone was in place at 10:00 a.m. The bailiff called for the jury to enter.

Judge El-Bib said, "Mr. Devas, please call your next witness."

Mr. Devas replied, "Yes, Your Honor. I call Dr. Lamb to the stand."

The bailiff swore in the witness.

Mr. Devas said to the witness, "Good morning, Dr. Lamb. Please tell us a little about yourself, your education, and your profession. What can you tell us about the Bible? Or what qualifies you to be an expert witness today?"

Dr. Lamb replied, "I am sixty-six years old. My wife died of cancer in 2015 at the young age of sixty, and we have no children. I have doctorate degrees in apologetics and geological science, and a master's degree in theology, all from the University of South Western (USW). While going to school at USW, I learned that Jesus is our Creator, our God, and the Savior of all people. Since my graduation thirty-six years ago, I have worked for the University of South Western in the field of Bible authority, with a large part based on apologetics. This is where I learned at a young age that Jesus is our Creator, God, and also the Savior of all people.

IS THE BIBLE NECESSARY?

"In my thirty-six years, I have reviewed various versions of the Bible. All the versions I consider to be perfect to a great extent because the archaeological digs have found not just evidence but, in many places, proof of the Bible's inerrancy. I have been and am presently an associate in many archaeological digs. You, the jury, have heard similar information from other witnesses about how perfect the Bible is."

Mr. Devas said, "Dr. Lamb, please describe in detail what apologetics is and how it affects the Bible and thus everyone in the world."

"Apologetics is a branch of theology devoted to the defense of the divine origin and authority of Christianity and the study of God's relation to the world. Apologetics covers a wide range of subjects, including the existence of God, evidence for the resurrection, evil, cults, science, etc. Apologetics is the religious discipline of defending religious doctrines through systematic argumentation and discourse. Early Christian writers who defended their beliefs against critics and recommended their faith to outsiders were called Christian apologists.

"We live in an age of rapid change and movement. Faddish trends appear one day and promptly vanish into obsolescence the next. Today, many discussions about postmodernism would likely fall into this category. Flooding the discussion with books and articles either decrying or defending postmodernism, many authors have set their sights on continuing this furious battle of tug-of-war. Meanwhile, large segments of the younger generation are growing apathetic toward the discussion. Nevertheless, the prevalence of postmodern thought accounts for a shift in the way people see truth. Although this shift has affected many areas of life in our culture, it has had a potent effect on believers in Christ particularly, with apathy toward learning and practicing apologetics among young believers.

"Ladies and gentlemen of the jury, the first witness, Dr. Lios, spoke to you in great detail about archaeology. We are fortunate to live in a time of history that is so very rich in archaeological discoveries and Bible translations that we are sure are the exact Word of God. I would like to add two additional excavations to Dr. Lios's list. First, in 1902, John Peters found a tomb with an inscription of 'Maresha,' a town mentioned in Joshua 15:44. It was once claimed that there was no Assyrian king named Sargon, as recorded in Isaiah 20:1, because this name was not known in any other record. Then Sargon's palace (627 BC) was discovered in Khorsabad, Iraq, in 1853. The very event mentioned in Isaiah 20, his capture of Ashdod, was recorded on the palace walls. What is more, fragments of a stela memorializing the victory were found at Ashdod itself. (A stela is an upright pillar bearing an inscription.)

"Undoubtedly one of the most important writings about Israel found, outside the Bible, is that on the Merneptah, or Israel, Stele. Discovered by Flinders Petrie in 1896, in Merneptah's mortuary temple in Thebes, one line mentions Israel: 'Israel is laid waste, its seed is not.' Here we have the earliest mention of Israel outside the Bible and the only mention of Israel in Egyptian records."

Mr. Devas asked, "Who wrote the first books of the Bible? And when?"

Dr. Lamb replied, "Job wrote the book of Job, and Moses wrote the first five books, called the Pentateuch, during the end of the Exodus, with the inspiration from God the Holy Spirit."

"How do we know that people could write so long ago?"

"Some scholars once claimed that the Mosaic Law could not have been written by Moses, because writing was largely unknown at that time and because the law of the Pentateuch was too sophisticated for that period. But the codified laws of Hammurabi (1700 BC), the Lipit-Ishtar Code (1860 BC), the Laws of Eshnunna (1950 BC), and the even earlier Ur-Nammu Code have refuted these claims. The Code of Ur-Nammu is the oldest known law surviving today. It was written on tablets in the Sumerian language (2100–2050 BC). These archaeological discoveries provide helpful external evidence of numerous other biblical details from the Old Testament, from Genesis to Ezra to Daniel. (Note: The Tower of Babel was built around 2200 BC.)"

Mr. Devas asked, "Would you speak on other subjects within apologetics?"

Dr. Lamb answered, "Yes, let's take science for example. Instead of science disproving the Bible, the Bible instead proves science. Parts of today's science books will be completely outdated next year, yet

IS THE BIBLE NECESSARY?

the Bible still stands as an accurate record of scientific facts, having never been changed. In the book of Job, which many consider to be the oldest book in the Bible, it is stated in Job 38:24, 'Minute light is divided [diffused].' This was proclaimed thousands of years before the discovery of splitting the light spectrum (1665). And again, in verse 31, God talks about 'binding the cluster of the seven stars [Pleiades 1610],' which was recently discovered to possibly be the center of gravitational pull for us in the Milky Way Galaxy. In that same verse, God mentions the 'Belt of Orion,' which we now know does indeed travel in a belt.

"Also, in **Job 40:15–17 (NKJV)**, it says, 'Look now at the behemoth, which I made along with you; He eats grass like an ox. See now, his strength is in his hips, and his power is in his stomach muscles. He moves his tail like a cedar; the sinews of his thighs are tightly knit.' Please look at the picture on the monitor, which is also on your computer. That's a picture, drawn in a cave, of a dinosaur that obviously lived at the same time as man. Has there been another animal with a tail the size of a cedar tree? Could this be the behemoth?"

Mr. Devas asked, "Do you have information about additional scientific facts in the Bible?"

"The chart on the monitor and in your computer shows scientific facts and principles that were in the Bible long before scientists discovered those scientific principles on earth. The Dead Sea Scrolls, historical documentation, and other sources all confirm the authenticity of the Bible. The Bible is estimated to have been written between 1500 BC and AD 100. People had no official knowledge of these scientific facts until more than a thousand years after the Bible was written. Isn't this scientific proof that the Bible verifies science? And that the Bible was inspired by God the Holy Spirit?"

Scientific fact or principle	Bible reference	Date of discovery
Air has weight.	Job 28:25	Sixteenth century
The earth is round.	Isaiah 40:22	Fifteenth century
Oceans have natural paths in them.	Psalm 8:8	1854
Both man and woman possess the seed of life.	Genesis 3:15	Seventeenth century
There is a place void of stars in the north.	Job 26:7	Nineteenth century
Earth is held in place by invisible forces.	Job 26:7	1650
Matter is made up of invisible particles.	Romans 1:20	Twentieth century
Certain animals carry diseases harmful to man.	Leviticus 11	Sixteenth century
There was an early diagnosis of leprosy.	Leviticus 13	Seventeenth century
The method of quarantine is effective for disease control.	Leviticus 13	Seventeenth century
The blood of animals carries diseases.	Leviticus 17	Seventeenth century
Blood is necessary for life.	Leviticus 17:11	Nineteenth century

IS THE BIBLE NECESSARY?

Lightning and thunder are related.	Job 38:25	Nineteenth century
The most seaworthy ship design ratio is 30:5:3.	Genesis 6	1860
Light is a particle and has mass (a photon).	Job 38:19	1932
Radio astronomy exists (stars give off signals).	Job 38:7	1945
Oceans contain freshwater springs.	Job 38:16	1920
Snow has material value.	Job 38:22	1905, 1966
An infinite number of stars exist.	Genesis 15:5	1940
Dust is important for survival.	Isaiah 40:12	1935
Human beings were the last living things created.	Genesis 1	Fifteenth century
Light can be split up into component colors.	Job 38:24	1650
Winds blow in cyclones.	Ecclesiastes 1:6	1836
Plants use sunlight to manufacture food.	Job 8:16	1920
Arcturus and other stars move through space.	Job 38:32	Nineteenth century
Water has a cycle.	Ecclesiastes 1:7	Seventeenth century

Dr. Lamb continued, "I will mention just one example, of which you are all familiar. The second one down, the fact that the earth is really round. Do any of you not believe that the earth is round? The Bible is scientifically accurate."

Mr. Devas said, "Please explain how the bombardier beetle is an example of irreducible complexity and how it is impossible to have come about through evolution."

"**Irreducible complexity** is just a fancy term used to mean a single system that is composed of several interacting parts, where the removal of any one of the parts causes the system to cease functioning. Thus, it could never have come together one part at a time, so it could never have evolved.

"**Bombardier beetles** eject a liquid called benzoquinone, which they superheat and expel in an intense pulsating jet. The explosive mechanism used by the beetle generates a spray that's much hotter than that of other insects that use the liquid, and it propels the jet five times faster. Yet it does not harm the beetle. A picture is on the monitor."

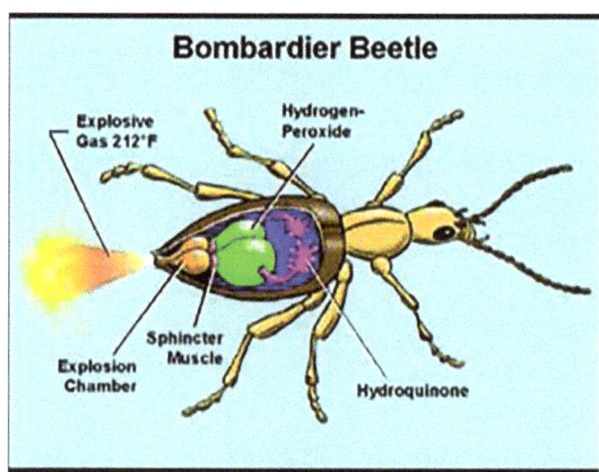

Mr. Devas asked, "Is the Bible inspired and inerrant?"

Dr. Lamb answered, "For us to know that God's Word is inspired and inerrant, we must first understand more fully what has been written. His Word was written for all men and for all ages, about Jesus, God the Son, and His creation. Jesus said in **Matthew 5:18–19 (NKJV)**, 'For assuredly, I say to you, till heaven and earth pass away, one jot or one tittle will by no means pass from the law till all is fulfilled. Whoever therefore breaks one of the least of these commandments, and teaches men so, shall be called least in the kingdom of heaven; but whoever does and teaches them, he shall be called great in the kingdom of heaven.' Throughout history and especially in recent modern times, man has tried to disprove God's Holy Word, the Bible. And yet each time an attack is made on it, God's Word always comes through the battle as the undefeated champion. The Bible is for everyone. Further, to correctly present God's Word to another individual can be very inspiring and motivating."

Mr. Devas turned to the judge. "That's all I have for this witness, Your Honor."

Judge El-Bib said, "Your questions, Mr. Cobra."

Mr. Cobra replied, "Thank you, Your Honor. Dr. Lamb, that behemoth you mentioned does not look anything like the dinosaurs that have been restructured from fossils from a million years ago. What do you say?"

Dr. Lamb answered, "First of all, I believe the earth is only six thousand years old. And, yes, the restructured dinosaurs you have seen may very well resemble an original, as they are described in Job 40:15–17 in the Bible. The picture of the dinosaur I showed earlier obviously lived at the same time as man. Otherwise, who drew the picture in the cave? Has there been another animal with a tail the size of a cedar tree? Could this be the behemoth?"

"You mentioned earlier that Jesus is our Creator, God, and also the Savior of all people. I can't believe that story. Do you believe in three gods?"

"No! It's just one God in three persons or entities. It's the Trinity."

"I don't understand. Do you have a simple explanation?"

Dr. Lamb answered, "We can use a Trinity concept for man. Man is three in one. He is mind, body, and spirit, but he is just one man. It's one of God's great mysteries."

"I don't believe any of that comparison to a god, and I don't believe others will either. Now can you prove that the universe didn't begin through evolution?"

"No, because the formation of the universe obviously can't be repeated. However, the evidence is so great that many scientists are convinced it was created. Many scientists agree that there was something or someone that somehow formed the estimated 26 sextillion planets (stars) that exist today. I only have one question: where did that something or someone come from? The Bible tells us in **Genesis 1:16 (NKJV)**, 'Then God made two great lights: the greater light to rule the day, and the lesser light to rule the night. He made the stars also.' The Bible is an essential book for everyone."

Mr. Cobra then asked, "So are you apologizing for the Bible with this apologetics?"

Dr. Lamb replied, "Not at all. Apologetics means 'a systematic argumentative discourse that is formal and orderly and usually an extended expression of thought on a subject.' Apologetics is used as a guide to help explain the details that are in the Bible. As I said before, apologetics is a branch of theology devoted to the defense of the divine origin and authority of Christianity, and it covers a wide range of subjects."

Mr. Cobra said to the judge, "I have nothing more for this witness."

Judge El-Bib asked, "Mr. Devas, do you have any additional questions?"

Mr. Devas replied, "No, sir."

Judge El-Bib told Dr. Lamb that he may step down, and he thanked him for his testimony. Then he pounded his gavel and instructed everyone to reconvene after lunch, at 2:00 p.m.

CHAPTER 18

PRIME MINISTER JEAN BERNARD THE BIBLE HELPS

Everyone was in place at 2:00 p.m. The bailiff called for the jury to enter.

Judge El-Bib said, "Mr. Devas, please call your next witness."

Mr. Devas called for Dr. Jean Bernard, our fifth witness, to come forward, and the bailiff swore in the witness. Mr. Devas then asked Dr. Jean Bernard to give details concerning himself and his profession.

Dr. Bernard replied, "I am fifty-three years old, and I am the Prime Minister of France. I have been married for twenty-six years, and our only child died six years ago, at the age of seventeen. I will not go into the duties of my profession because I am here for a completely different reason, which is to speak in defense of the Bible.

"I must give you a few details of my life. I was born and raised in Paris, France, and I have a brother and a sister. My parents raised the three of us in what might be called a normal family. My mother and father did not follow any particular religion, and thus, we were raised not knowing any faith system. It wasn't until I was in the sixth grade that I heard some of my friends speak about different religions, like Christianity, Buddhism, etc. Since my parents spoiled us, I had an easygoing childhood. The thought of religion never entered my mind through high school.

"About four years after acquiring a law degree and working as a lawyer, I met a beautiful young lady named Caroline, who became my wife soon after. At that same time, I felt something was missing in my life at the age of twenty-seven. At that time, I became friends with a few people in the law firm where I worked, including a fellow by the name of Bob, who was a Christian. One day he asked me straightforward if I knew anything about the Bible and Jesus Christ. I was startled by the question and did not respond. But Bob persisted and asked if we could get together some evening and talk. I agreed, and we set a date for the following week. That evening started a whole new chapter in the lives of my wife and me."

Mr. Devas said, "Please tell us, Mr. Prime Minister, how, when, and why your life changed."

Dr. Jean Bernard said, "Ladies and gentlemen, you have had previous witnesses inform you in great detail about the truth of the Bible. I'm here to explain how the Bible is a necessity today in your world and mine. My life and my wife's are not isolated cases. There are literally millions of people around the world who have needed—and I repeat, needed—the comfort, peace, love, and wisdom found in the Bible.

"For my wife and me, there were several times in our lives where Christ and the Bible provided wisdom and guidance in difficult times. I will only mention two.

First, "Years ago, our family had some serious financial problems, to the point that we were losing our business. We put it on the market for six months, but it did not sell. We consulted our friend Bob, who simply reminded us that the business and the money it represents belong to Jesus. So he advised us to emotionally let the business go. The Lord would sell it in His time. We fervently prayed about it for two weeks, and the business was sold within that two-week period. The Bible tells us to pray constantly about everything.

Second, "My wife had decided years ago to be a stay-at-home wife and mother. About six years ago, a few months after I was elected prime minister, we experienced a terrible family tragedy. Our daughter died from a rare disease. Soon after our daughter died, my wife became clinically depressed. To make a long story short, at one point a few months later, she was on our bed with the Bible on her chest, and it was opened to **Matthew 28:26 (NKJV)**, which reads, 'I am with you always, even to the end of the age.' As soon as she read that verse, she sat up, closed the Bible, and called me at work. She said, 'Can you get off early? We're going to celebrate.' She told me the whole story at dinner that evening. Her depression had lifted almost immediately after reading the verse.

"I know the jury has information about the Bible on their computers in their hotel rooms. But whether this trial lasts a few days or weeks, that's not enough time to share with you even a small portion of the promises of God that are in the Bible. With that said, please consider for a moment, if you will, that Jesus is your Creator, God, and Savior, and that the Bible is His love letter to each of us personally. What are the alternatives?

"My wife and I pray about our problems and read particular and pertinent verses that are in the Bible, like the ones on the monitors, which bring us comfort. In the Bible, **John 16:30–33 (NKJV)** says, '"Now we are sure that You know all things, and have no need that anyone should question You. By this we believe that You came forth from God." Jesus answered them, "Do you now believe? Indeed the hour is coming, yes, has now come, that you will be scattered, each to his own, and will leave Me alone. And yet I am not alone, because the Father is with Me. These things I have spoken to you, that in Me you may have peace. In the world you will have tribulation; but be of good cheer, I have overcome the world."' We have all had trouble of some kind in our lives. But I know that Jesus oversees all that I do.

"Many people have heard of the twenty-third psalm. **Psalm 23:4 (NKJV)** says, 'Yea, though I walk through the valley of the shadow of death, I will fear no evil; For You are with me; Your rod and Your staff, they comfort me.' The rod and staff are items a shepherd uses to guide his sheep. Jesus uses His quiet voice and the Bible as the rod and the staff to guide us.

"**Philippians 4:6–8 (NKJV)** says, 'Be anxious for nothing, but in everything by prayer and supplication, with thanksgiving, let your requests be made known to God; and the peace of God, which surpasses all understanding, will guard your hearts and minds through Christ Jesus. Finally, brethren, whatever things are true, whatever things are noble, whatever things are just, whatever things are pure, whatever things are lovely, whatever things are of good report, if there is any virtue and if there is anything praiseworthy—meditate on these things.'" After a short pause, Dr. Jean Bernard continued. "How can the Bible be considered a great depravity, an atrocity, stupid and cruel, when it obviously emphasizes so many wonderful values, like hope, love, and those I just mentioned?"

Mr. Devas said, "Mr. Prime Minister, please tell the jury what you previously shared with me concerning the words of Jesus."

Dr. Jean Bernard replied, "Why do I, as a Christian, tell people about Jesus? I hope you will understand this word picture. Consider the water in the following illustration to be the WORDS of Jesus. High above is a picturesque mountain full of snow. Now picture the snow melting and cool water flowing into a few streams and then into a beautiful large lake about one mile across. The lake is overflowing with deep blue water that is swarming with fish and gorgeous vegetation all around. From high above come gorgeous birds of all colors and species, which land smoothly on the lake and the shore. The water from the lake then flows down into a beautiful river with lush foliage on both sides. There are many tributaries from this river that feed the countryside and then join back to the one large river. It would be good if the water flowed to the ocean, but it does not. It flows into another lake with no outlet. What happens to that water? It gets stagnant. It will support no life, except maybe bacteria and algae.

"The word picture I'm sharing with you came to me from a friend I met eleven years ago. He showed me why Jesus Christ and the Bible are so important to me and everyone. So as the water from the mountain brings life, so do the words from Jesus and the Bible bring life. That information flows through me like the water in the river. But I must not allow this water (the words of Jesus) to become stagnant. I let it flow as I share it with others, just like I am sharing it with you. When Mr. Devas asked if I would be a witness at this trial,

IS THE BIBLE NECESSARY?

I said I definitely would because I must explain everything as Jesus has directed me to share."

Mr. Devas said, "Thank you, Mr. Prime Minister, for taking time out of what must be a very busy schedule. Do you have anything further?"

Dr. Jean Bernard replied, "Yes, I am sharing with you the necessity, in my mind, for all nations and people to know that the Bible teaches peace, love, and healthy relationships with others. Please remember, if you will, that this book, the Bible, is a love letter from Jesus Christ to you and me and all who live. Unlike what Mr. Cobra has said, no one has ever been hurt by reading the Bible. Even though the Bible contains some sad historical events and describes stories of flawed people, it has a lot to say about trusting God in order to achieve a life of fulfillment, a life of peace and love for God and one another. Jesus is called the Prince of Peace in Isaiah 9:6, and 1 John 4:8 (NKJV) says, 'He who does not love does not know God, for God is love.' Further, Paul refers to 'the God of all peace' in Romans 15:33.

"A word often translated, *peace* in the Bible actually means 'to tie together as a whole; when all essential parts are joined together.' Inner peace then is a wholeness of mind and spirit, a whole heart at rest, which comes from Jesus Christ. Inner peace has little to do with external surroundings. Jesus said in **John 14:27 (NKJV)**, 'Peace I leave with you, My peace I give to you; not as the world gives do I give to you. Let not your heart be troubled, neither let it be afraid.' So peace is not the absence of trouble. It is the presence of God (Jesus).

"We can have peace in the midst of challenges when we remember that **Romans 8:28 (NKJV)** says, 'And we know that all things work together for good to those who love God, to those who are the called according to His purpose.' We can choose peace rather than give way to fear and worry. Inner peace resulting from a relationship with Jesus allows us to keep things in proper perspective. We can accept difficult situations on earth by remembering that our citizenship is in heaven, and we also know that close family and friends can help (Philippians 3:20).

"Jesus said, 'Blessed are the peacemakers, for they will be called sons of God' **(Matthew 5:9 NKJV)**.

"God's desire is that we who know Him learn to live in peace within ourselves first. Then we can radiate that peace to others, bringing calmness and wisdom to tense situations, and in so doing, be a light in the world so others can see 'the Way' (Matthew 5:14; Philippians 2:14–15)."

Mr. Devas said, "Thank you, Mr. Prime Minister. Your Honor, I have nothing further for this witness at this time. However, I would like to reserve the right to call him back at a later time."

Judge El-Bib said, "Very well, Mr. Devas. Mr. Cobra, your witness."

Mr. Cobra stood up. "Thank you, Your Honor. Mr. Prime Minister, good morning, sir. Tell us, were you elected to your position, or were you appointed?"

Mr. Devas said, "I object, Your Honor. How is that relevant to the case?"

Judge El-Bib said, "Objection sustained. Be careful, Mr. Cobra."

Mr. Cobra replied, "I'm sorry, Your Honor. Mr. Prime Minister, how long have you been in your present position?"

Dr. Jean Bernard replied, "I have been prime minister for six years."

"You talk about peace. You mention the peace from Christ. But I don't see any peace in the world at all. All I see is trouble, doubt, fighting, and wars. Where is the peace?"

"Doubt and trouble are experiences common to all people. Even those with faith in Jesus struggle with doubt and have trouble on occasion. The man in Mark 9:24 (NKJV) made a comment to Jesus: 'Lord, I believe; help my unbelief.' Some people are hindered greatly by doubt. Some see it as a springboard to life. The Bible has something to say about the cause of doubt and provides examples of people who struggled with it.

"Zechariah was visited by an angel of the Lord and was told that he would have a son. He doubted God's ability to overcome natural obstacles. He thought he and his wife were too old. Many people today share the same doubt. Any time we allow human reason to overshadow faith in God, sinful doubt and strife can result. No matter how logical our reasons may seem, God has made foolish the wisdom of the world (1 Corinthians 1:20), and His seemingly foolish plans are far wiser than man's. Faith is trusting God even when His plan goes against human reason or experience. You may have doubt about a subject, but then your mind comes up with an opinion. Then hopefully, reason is followed by facts and evidence and then sometimes proof. So even though some of your thoughts may start with doubt, that is okay. Allow doubt to expand in your thought process. If you are struggling to make a decision or are struggling with what to believe, seek God's counsel through prayer, and His Word and peace will come to you."

Mr. Cobra asked, "Isn't it true that the unfortunate events or circumstances that have happened to you and your family could've been resolved naturally and not by using the Bible?"

Dr. Jean Bernard replied, "I am as convinced as I am sitting here that the Bible was the primary factor providing the resolution of our difficulties. We believe that the Bible is perfect, which means, of course, that all information in it is true. I am a student of the Bible, and if I may, I would like to quote one more Bible verse that will explain clearly what I am referring to."

"I don't believe that will be necessary."

Mr. Devas called out, "Objection, Your Honor. The witness should be able to explain in detail his thoughts on the subject."

Judge El-Bib said, "Objection sustained. Please continue, Mr. Prime Minister."

Dr. Jean Bernard continued, "In my professional position, I have reviewed surveys and questionnaires that ask the general public what they really want in life. It seems that it can all be broken down in a few words. Faith, hope (for peace), love (for God and neighbor), and also justice and mercy in our spiritual and secular lives are the considerations that people want most. Further, man IS a spiritual being. What do we expect spiritually from life? It seems simple, but countries, cultures, and even fathers and sons don't agree on some simple matters. So what's the answer?

"The Bible says in 1 Corinthians 13:13 (NKJV), 'And now abide faith, hope, love, these three; but the greatest of these is love.' The Bible is definitely needed in the world."

Mr. Cobra said, "You said that the Bible has wisdom. Wisdom is defined as 'the ability to discern inner qualities and relationships.' You said, and I quote, 'the comfort and the wisdom found in the Bible.' How can an inert thing have inner qualities and relationships? Only humans have those qualities."

Dr. Jean Bernard replied, "There are books on law, automobile mechanics, and the like. These books do not **do** anything on their own, but they guide the reader to apply the information that is in the book to gain knowledge in the subject matter investigated, which leads to understanding and eventually wisdom."

Mr. Cobra turned and said, "I have nothing more for this witness."

Judge El-Bib asked, "Mr. Devas, do you have any additional questions?"

Mr. Devas replied, "No, sir, but thank you."

Judge El-Bib directed Dr. Bernard to step down from the witness box and thanked him for his answers. He pounded his gavel and instructed everyone to reconvene tomorrow morning at 10:00 a.m.

CHAPTER 19

DR. MARY GRAVES
WHY JESUS

Judge El-Bib said, "Mr. Devas, please call your next witness." The time was 10:00 a.m.

Mr. Devas said, "At this time, Your Honor, I would like the discussion to be about the truth or fiction of Bible history. I would like to call our sixth witness to the stand Dr. Mary Graves. She is an expert in the history of ancient times."

The bailiff swore in the witness.

Mr. Devas said, "Good morning, Dr. Graves. Tell us a little about yourself and your study of people in history, especially Jesus Christ."

Dr. Mary Graves replied, "Good morning. First, I would like to mention to the judge that you have approved all the Bible verses I will put on the monitors."

Judge El-Bib said, "Very well. Please continue."

Dr. Graves said, "Thank you. I am married to a wonderful man, and we have three children. Sometime during my testimony, I would like to share with you one instance of how biblical teachings contributed to our strong marriage. I have thirty-five years' experience in historical studies, covering the period of 2500 BC (Noah and the flood) to AD 1600 (the Reformation). I have doctorate degrees in ancient history and theology from Harvest University, with studies emphasizing the time and the life of Jesus Christ."

Mr. Devas said, "Before you tell us about Jesus, please tell us about one famous person or event in Bible history."

"To be honest, for centuries, people have scoffed at the idea that David of the Bible could've killed a giant like Goliath with a stone. This is the same David who not only became the king of Israel but is in the genealogy of Jesus.

"Well, I'm here to tell you that in my studies of ancient history, I have discovered interesting information about stone slingers. Believe it or not, as a child, young David was the shepherd of his family's flock of sheep. They certainly didn't have guns three thousand years ago, and at that time in history, the area we now call Israel had lions and bears. So what did David use to protect his sheep? What is faster than a speeding bullet and more powerful than a locomotive? While slingstones do not quite meet that standard, they were nonetheless among the most important deadly weapons in an ancient army's arsenal.

"So what about the narrative concerning David and Goliath? Goliath was a giant of a man, standing some nine feet tall, from an adjacent nation at war with Israel. Could a young lad, David, possibly strike down a warrior the size and strength of Goliath? The answer is yes! The Bible mentions slingers, like in Judges 20:15–16, 1 Samuel 17:14, and 2 Chronicles 26:14. These verses verify one event that gives us strong evidence and even some proof that historical events written in the Bible are true. Also, modern-day newspapers and magazines have articles about slingers being used in battle in today's hostile conflicts. See the pictures on the monitors. In an archaeological excavation ten miles north of Jerusalem, in Israel's West Bank, slingstones have been found in almost all the digs."

A warrior in present-day Palestine slinging a stone.

Roman lead sling bullets. This is a deadly weapon used even in today's world.

Mr. Devas said, "You have mentioned to me how the Bible has helped your marriage. Please explain."

Dr. Graves replied, "When my husband and I had been dating for about four months, we did a lot of kissing and petting. At one point, we both felt we wanted to be closer, but we knew it wasn't right to get more intimate. The Bible mentions that in detail. So we talked it over and made a plan that didn't allow us to be in a place where we might give in to our desires. That worked. That made us both extremely happy and proud on our wedding day."

"Are there any secular folks who mention Jesus?"

"There are many. Your Honor, may I read about one of the historical writers who mention Christ? Mr. Cobra, you have a copy."

Judge El-Bib said, "Please continue."

Dr. Graves continued. "Tacitus (AD 56–120) wrote, 'Consequently, to get rid of the report [about Jesus's followers], Nero fastened the guilt and inflicted the most exquisite [excruciating] tortures on a class hated for their abominations, called Christians by the populace. Christ, from whom the name had its origin, suffered the extreme penalty during the reign of Tiberius at the hands of one of our procurators, Pontius Pilatus, and a most mischievous superstition, thus checked for the moment, again broke out not only in Judea, the first source of the evil, but even in Rome, where all things hideous and shameful from every part of the world find their center and become popular.' And like I said, there are many more people who wrote about Jesus."

Mr. Devas said, "Now please speak about Jesus."

"Before we discuss Jesus and the question of whether He is God, we should ask ourselves these questions. Is there a god? What is the evidence to prove it?

"'Is there a god?' is among the most basic questions asked by human beings. For the majority of history, the overwhelming answer to this question has been yes, though there have been strong discords (lack of agreement) about what kind of god or gods exist. There are plenty of reasons to believe in God. The real question is whether or not a person is open to this evidence."

IS THE BIBLE NECESSARY?

Looking at the gallery, Dr. Graves asked, "Are you open to the evidence concerning Jesus, God the Son, and His book, the Bible? Some say, 'If God would show me a miracle, I would believe.' Should God be challenged? For example, 'I dare you, God, to put me in a new car.' You see, He just won't do that. A big part of knowing there is a God and believing in Him is faith (a firm belief in something for which there is no proof).

"There are some examples.

1. "The theory of relativity, which is almost universally accepted among scientists, has certain implications for this law of cause and effect. It is a relationship between events or things, where one is the result of the other or others. This is a combination of action and reaction. Something happens (a cause that leads to an effect). One is that the universe—defined as time, space, matter, and physical energy—had a beginning that is not eternal. This is faith!
2. "Science has proven that the universe really did have a beginning. This means that if the universe had a starting point in history, then it obviously began to exist. It must have a cause for its existence. Therefore, if the universe needs a cause for its coming into being, then that cause must be beyond the universe—which is time, space, matter, and physical energy. That cause must be something similar to what Christians call a Creator, 'God.' This is faith!
3. "There are an estimated 15 to 30 trillion cells in the body. If only one entity somehow began with two cells and they doubled every year, it would take thirty years just to accumulate one billion cells, and that's only for one person. If no cells die, what is the probability of these cells becoming a human? There is a God! This is faith!"

Mr. Devas asked, "How does this God communicate with us? Which of our senses does He use? Does He speak to us in a whisper or in a regular voice? A vision? Or written means?"

Dr. Graves replied, "God speaks to us by His written Word, the Bible. But we must be open to what He has to say to us. 'Everyone would get the same message!' Okay, yes, it's in the Bible. However, their interpretation may be different.

"There is much evidence for the existence of God. Assessing evidence includes properly categorizing it. Some balk at the idea of 'evidence' for God the Father, who is invisible and immaterial. However, even hardened skeptics accept the meaningful existence of many such things, such as the laws of logic. Logic is neither material nor visible, yet it's legitimately considered real and can be both perceived and examined. One cannot see logic or mechanically quantify it, but this does not justify any useful claim that logic does not exist. The same is true, to varying degrees, with other concepts, such as morality, gravity, love, and hate.

"Perhaps the weakest response to evidence of God's existence is ignoring it—claiming there is no evidence. So is there any real proof for God? No. But again, what about the evidence? There is a lot of evidence. Remember, in today's courts, people are convicted of horrible crimes based on strong evidence even if there is no proof."

"Please give us an example of evidence for something that appears to be an unknown."

Dr. Graves answered, "For one example of evidence, allow me to summarize the evidence for cosmology with the following statements:

(1) *Whatever begins to exist must have a reason for its existence.*
(2) *The universe began to exist.*
(3) *Therefore, the universe must have a reason for its existence.*
(4) *The attributes of the reason for the universe (being timeless, existing outside of space, and so on) are the attributes of God.*
(5) *Therefore, the reason for the universe must be God, as the Bible says in Genesis 1:1 (NKJV), 'In the beginning God created the heavens and the earth.'*

"And with that evidence, everyone here can agree that there is a God. Now the question is, is Jesus God? Yes, He is!"

IS THE BIBLE NECESSARY?

Mr. Devas asked, "Is Jesus God? Why should I believe that Jesus is God?"

Dr. Graves replied, "Some who deny that Jesus is God make the claim that Jesus never said that He is God. It is correct that the Bible never records Jesus saying the precise words 'I am God.' This does not mean, however, that Jesus never claimed to be God. He did claim divine authority."

"Please explain."

"Matthew 26:63–65 (NKJV) says, 'And the high priest answered and said to Him [Jesus], "I put You under oath by the living God: Tell us if You are the Christ, the Son of God!" Jesus said to him, "It is as you said. Nevertheless, I say to you, hereafter you will see the Son of Man sitting at the right hand of the Power, and coming on the clouds of heaven." Then the high priest tore his clothes, saying, "He has spoken blasphemy! What further need do we have of witnesses?"'

"Also, in John 19:7–8 (NKJV), it says, 'The Jews answered him [Pilate], "We have a law, and according to our law He ought to die, because He made Himself the Son of God." Therefore, when Pilate heard that saying, he was the more afraid.' Why would His claiming to be the Son of God be considered blasphemy and be worthy of a death sentence? The Jewish leaders understood exactly what Jesus meant by the phrase 'Son of God.' To be the Son of God is to be of the same nature as God. The Son of God is God.

"Also, in the Bible, Mark 2:3–5 (NKJV) tells the story of Jesus healing a man with palsy because Jesus saw that the man had tremendous faith. 'Then they came to Him, bringing a paralytic who was carried by four men. And when they could not come near Him because of the crowd, they uncovered the roof where He was. So when they had broken through, they let down the bed on which the paralytic was lying. When Jesus saw their faith, He said to the paralytic, "Son, your sins are forgiven you."'

"Now let's say that today, in our world, some guy is walking down the street, and he comes upon a car accident. He walks up to the car and sees that the people in the car are badly injured. So he tells them their sins are forgiven. Wouldn't you think he's sick in the head? The stories are exactly the same, except that Jesus is God and does forgive sins and is the only One who can. So the Jewish leaders understood the message here and needed no more information. Jesus might as well have said, 'I am God.' So the leaders planned for Jesus's death, and in fact, they did have Him crucified. Further, Jesus overtly upheld belief in Old Testament historical events by quoting twenty-nine of them. By doing so, He magnified the fact that the whole of the Bible, His Book, was and is holy and without error.

"The cornerstone of Christian belief is the resurrection of Christ. Even Paul the Apostle stated as fact in **1 Corinthians 15:17 (NKJV)**, 'And if Christ has not been raised, your faith is futile; you are still in your sins.' In this sense, making a case for the truth of the resurrection also makes a case for the claims of Jesus and, in turn, the reliability, inerrancy, and truth of the Bible."

Mr. Devas asked, "What is the purpose of the Bible?"

Dr. Graves replied, "The Bible's purpose is twofold. The first is to show us that all have broken God's law. It's declared in **James 2:10 (NKJV)**, 'For whoever shall keep the whole law, and yet stumble in one point, he is guilty of all.' God's law reveals how all people have sinned against God and are deserving of the fullness of His judgment. That sounds tough, but Jesus has provided a path for all His children—everyone.

"The Bible is God's Word. If we have to speak of a single purpose of the Bible, it would be to reveal God to us. There are many things that we would never know about God unless He told them to us. The Bible is God's self-revelation to humanity.

"Second, the Bible tells us who we are and why we are here. It tells us of our sin and of God's plan of salvation in Jesus Christ (God the Son). Thus, we can all be saved and spared from a horrible eternal death. Then we will be able to join Jesus in paradise, which is heaven."

"What must we do to join Jesus in paradise?"

"This is where the Bible comes in. Obviously, we can't speak to Jesus face-to-face. So the Bible tells us exactly what to do. On the monitor are a few verses that pertain to salvation.

"**John 5:24 (NKJV)** says, 'Most assuredly, I say to you, he who hears My word and believes in Him who sent Me has everlasting life, and shall not come into judgment, but has passed from death into life.'

"**Philippians 2:12–13 (NKJV)** says, 'Work out your own salvation with fear and trembling; for it is God who works in you both to will and to do for His good pleasure.'

"And in **Ephesians 2:8–9 (NKJV)**, Paul says, 'For by grace you have been saved through faith, and that not of yourselves; it is the gift of God, not of works, lest anyone should boast.'

"So there you have it. It's simple."

Mr. Devas asked, "Is Jesus mentioned or referred to as God in the Bible?"

Dr. Graves answered, "Yes, many times. On the monitor are a few verses, and on the computers in your rooms is a chart showing many verses where Jesus is mentioned or referred to as God."

JESUS IS IN MOST EVERY BOOK OF THE BIBLE.

1 Thessalonians 1:1 (NKJV). "To the church of the Thessalonians in God the Father and the Lord Jesus Christ: Grace to you and peace from God our Father and the Lord Jesus Christ."

1 Kings 8:27 (NKJV). Jesus is the answer to the question. "But will God indeed dwell on the earth? Behold, heaven and the heaven of heavens cannot contain You. How much less this temple which I have built!" (Also John 1:14 and John 2:19.)

Joel 2:32 (NKJV). "And it shall come to pass that whoever calls on the name of the Lord shall be saved. For in Mount Zion and in Jerusalem there shall be deliverance, As the Lord has said, among the remnant whom the Lord calls." (Also Romans 10:13 and Acts 2:21.)

Mr. Devas asked, "What is Christianity?"

Dr. Graves replied, "I would like to talk about true Christianity. Many of you have heard the expression 'Try it. You'll like it.' That phrase certainly pertains to Christianity and the Bible. Let's say you decide to study the Bible. Most of your study probably would come from the Bible itself or commentaries, science books, and other Christians. By the way, Christianity is not a religion. It is a relationship with Jesus our Creator, God, and Savior, similar to a relationship with a parent or friend, but much closer and holy.

"Now granted, this study will take some time, but it will be worth it. Christianity can never be forced on people because only Jesus knows your heart. C. S. Lewis, in his book *Mere Christianity*, stated that Jesus was both a liar and a lunatic or Lord of all creation. In the Bible, the Lord Jesus left nothing in between to consider. I believe with all my heart that after a study of the Bible, most individuals who seek God with all their heart will determine that Christianity is the only way to God and eternity.

"Christianity began with the birth of Jesus Christ about 2020 years ago, give or take five years, in the town of Bethlehem. But before that, there were hundreds of prophecies in the Old Testament of the Bible concerning Jesus's birth and describing the events in His life. That cannot be a coincidence. Compare Christianity with any other religious philosophy in the world. Can all spiritual teachings be right? I don't think so. There are too many differences."

Mr. Devas turned to the judge. "That's all I have for this witness, Your Honor."

Judge El-Bib said, "Your questions, Mr. Cobra."

Mr. Cobra stood up. "Thank you, Your Honor. Dr. Graves, I will not argue that Jesus actually lived." There was a long pause. "However, I personally doubt it. But the Bible tells of many preposterous myths in Jesus's life, like walking on water, healing the blind, and raising the dead. An intelligent person simply cannot believe it. Some of the Bible is wrong. Isn't that so?"

Dr. Graves replied, "Archaeology has settled that question. There have been hundreds of biblical cities and thus events discovered by archaeologists. And as for the events in the life of Jesus, there were many eyewitnesses indicated in the New Testament of the Bible."

"Most references in the Bible are not about Jesus at all. Why not?"

"Jesus Christ Himself is the primary subject of the entire Bible. His name is mentioned or alluded to in almost every book of the Bible, as I put on the monitor a few minutes ago—"

Mr. Cobra interrupted and, looking at the jury, said, "I am showing a list of Bible verses on the monitor that are Bible contradictions. One, to enslave or not to enslave? Leviticus 25:45 and Isaiah 58:6. Two, is God all good or not? Numbers 23:19 and Exodus 32:14. Three, has anyone ever looked upon God's face? John 1:18 and Genesis 32:30. Please look at these verses during your deliberations. Sorry to interrupt. Please continue."

Dr. Graves said, "I will only comment on one. If Christ is correct, then Jacob did not wrestle with God the Father, but another person of the Trinity—either the preincarnate Christ (God the Son) or God the Holy Spirit. The word *trinity* is not in the Bible and is a mystery, but it is used to represent three persons in one God. A secular example of a trinity may be the sun. The sun gives us (1) heat, (2) light, and (3) gravity. For another example, a human is mind, body, and spirit. But these do not adequately explain the mystery of the Trinity of God.

"It is amazing that Jesus did not physically write one word of the Bible, but inspired forty authors to compose this marvelous *love letter* from Him to all of us. There are sixty-six books and almost one million words in the Bible. *All the books in the Bible are necessary in order to tell the full history.* If it can be shown that the four gospels, Matthew, Mark, Luke, and John, present an accurate account of the life and ministry of Jesus, then Jesus Himself becomes the main contention in support of the truth of the Bible—that Jesus is God.

"For the jury's assistance, there is a book on their computers titled *The Testimony of the Evangelists*, written by Simon Greenleaf. That book covers the gospels of Matthew, Mark, Luke, and John. Matthew and John were eyewitnesses for three and a half years in the life of Jesus, up to his death on the cross. Luke was a doctor who followed Jesus's life and works. He questioned dozens, maybe hundreds, of people concerning the life of Jesus. That's why he said in **Luke 1:1–4 (NKJV)**, 'Inasmuch as many have taken in hand to set in order a narrative of those things which have been fulfilled among us, just as those who from the beginning were eyewitnesses and ministers of the word delivered them to us, it seemed good to me also, having had perfect understanding of all things from the very first, to write to you an orderly account, most excellent Theophilus, that you may know the certainty of those things in which you were instructed.' Theophilus was a high priest from Antioch. As for the Gospel of Mark, church fathers state that Mark was the interpreter for Peter, which would give reason to believe that he wrote the Gospel of Mark under the guidance and assistance of the apostle Peter."

Mr. Cobra said, "Okay, another subject! Nice story about the slinger, but it is just a fable. I don't believe your fairy tale about the slingers. You say a thirteen-year-old kid can hurl a rock so hard as to knock down a giant? At this time, Your Honor, I am requesting that one of my staff come forward. He is wearing a warrior's headpiece, as they did four thousand years ago."

Judge El-Bib said, "I'll allow it."

Mr. Cobra then said, "Please note the small space between the eyes. How could a boy possibly kill a giant man with a stone?"

Dr. Graves answered, "Yes, a slinger could kill a person with one shot with accuracy and range. In the Roman army, a well-trained slinger was considered equal to an equally trained bowman. The slingers had an advantage in more power per shot, regularly smashing bones without any visible damage to the skin and being far cheaper. But research published in *National Geographic* showed that a slingshot used by the Romans some 1,900 years ago had nearly the same stopping power as a pistol. In the hands of an expert, a heavy sling bullet or stone could reach speeds of up to 100 mph. The biggest slingstones were very powerful. These were shown on the monitor."

"The Bible mentions many miracles. Can you convince us they are true?"

Dr. Graves replied, "MIRACLES! In the Old Testament, God parted the Red Sea, allowing His people to escape a hoard of angry

Egyptians. In the book of Joshua, the sun stood still. There were other miracles. In the New Testament, the blind received sight, and the lame walked. Jesus walked on water and was resurrected from the dead after being executed on a cross. Miracles are obviously a one-time event and cannot be repeated like in a laboratory experiment.

"In a largely naturalistic age, meaning that belief is only in the material world, miracles are often disregarded as nonsense. The supernatural—anything beyond the natural world—is dismissed or relegated to a second-class status. This often results in doubt, but from doubt, your mind can and will develop an opinion on the subject matter. Then you will be able to develop a reason that will lead to facts and evidence. Can we trust it to be true? Are we really expected to believe the supernatural events the Bible records? Are we to dismiss miracles out of existence rather than reasoning and developing answers that if God exists—and I just showed you that He does—then miracles are possible?

"Throughout recorded history, ordinary people have witnessed miracles and reported them. Now in my personal experience, from about 1985 to 1993, my husband and I attended a Bible-believing church that had a missionary outreach. After one of the pastors—let's call him James—returned from a mission trip to India, he shared his adventures with us. He told of a meeting with some village leaders when one leader—let's call him Pete—showed up an hour late, which was very unusual. After the meeting, our pastor James curiously asked Pete why he was late. Pete said he had just returned from a small village where about 40 percent of the people were very sick from a worldwide virus. Without hesitation, he said, 'I cured ten people in the first village, and in the second village, I raised one man from the dead and healed four others who were sick.'

"Pastor James instantly stopped him because he was so surprised by what Pastor Pete had said so matter-of-factly. He asked Pastor Pete if he had actually raised somebody from the dead. Pete said, 'Yes. Do you not do that in the United States?' Pastor James was beside himself with disbelief, yet he truly believed that Pastor Pete had raised a man from the dead. Pastor Pete reminded us that Jesus told His Apostles in **John 14:12 (NKJV)**, 'Most assuredly, I say to you, he who believes in Me, the works that I do he will do also; and greater works than these he will do, because I go to My Father.'

"What does 'greater' mean? 'Greater' means 'more numerous' or 'more widely dispersed.' In that sense, Christians have indeed done greater things than Jesus did. Christians have preached all around the world and have seen millions of men and women converted. Pastor James prayed to the Lord to help his unbelief, as have my husband and I many times."

Mr. Cobra stated, laughing, "Your Honor, this witness is a complete liar. This story is completely absurd. I have no more questions for this witness. I object, and I request that her entire testimony be stricken from the record."

Judge El-Bib said, "Objection denied." He turned to the other lawyer. "Mr. Devas?"

Mr. Devas replied, "No, thank you, Your Honor, and thank you, Dr. Graves, for your splendid testimony. At this time, the defense rests."

Judge El-Bib pounded his gavel and instructed everyone to reconvene tomorrow morning at 10:00 for the closing statements.

CHAPTER 20

Mr. Cobra's Closing Statement

It was 10:00 a.m. The jury and attorneys were in the courtroom. The judge had just entered the courtroom and had taken his seat.

Judge El-Bib said, "The judge asks Mr. Cobra to make his closing statement."

Mr. Cobra walked toward the jury and said, "As I said in my opening statement, I believe that you are all too smart to accept that the Bible is from some god. You know that it is full of errors, contradictions, and unbelievable myths and stories. We have shown that the Bible is no more than a crutch needed by people too weak to stand on their own. You will easily come to the conclusion that the Bible is guilty as charged and is not to be printed anywhere in the world. Mr. Devas and his witnesses have shown you some colorful pictures on the monitor, but—" He paused. "They are inconsequential.

"It's up to you, the jury, to look past the fog of so-called evidence that Mr. Devas has presented. Your guilty verdict will ensure that the world is free of this written dictator. The Bible also has a lot of writing that is quite disturbing, like the following example: Judges 1:1–4 (NKJV). 'Now after the death of Joshua it came to pass that the children of Israel asked the Lord, saying, "Who shall be first to go up for us against the Canaanites to fight against them?" And the Lord said, "Judah shall go up. Indeed I have delivered the land into his hand." So Judah said to Simeon his brother, "Come up with me to my allotted territory, that we may fight against the Canaanites; and I will likewise go with you to your allotted territory." And Simeon went with him. Then Judah went up, and the Lord delivered the Canaanites and the Perizzites into their hand; and they killed ten thousand men at Bezek.'

"Children should not read or be subjected to verses like the one I just read. 'What profit has a man from all his labor in which he toils under the sun? One generation passes away, and another generation comes; But the earth abides forever. The sun also rises, and the sun goes down, and hastens to the place where it arose. The wind goes toward the south, and turns around to the north; the wind whirls about continually, and comes again on its circuit.' The activity of people is included in this observation that all things produce only indescribable weariness and lack of satisfaction. 'That which has been is what will be, That which is done is what will be done, And there is nothing new under the sun' (Ecclesiastes 1:9 NKJV).

"The Bible is prejudiced, favoring certain groups of people over others. Just look at all the people the Hebrews slaughtered in the name of their god! And with their god's blessing! How can the earth have peace and love when this book condoned slaughtering whole nations in the Old Testament?

"We all want peace and love for the whole world. What is the best way to achieve this goal? You may not know that the Universal Senate of World Religions has many groups working on a solution. The more people agree on a subject matter, the better one's day-to-day needs and respect for one another will be met. The way to do that is for groups of like-minded neighbors, friends, communities, and governmental entities to join together and then encourage other activists to join. These are steps that the Universal Senate of World Religions is taking right now.

"Members of the jury, you can see how and why the Bible is no longer needed. The world can solve its own problems without the Bible's narrow-minded demands and opinions. It is simply too outdated and old-fashioned to be relevant in today's world. Relegate it to the trash heap, where it belongs.

"Dr. Winter said that in his view—and I agree—humanism/atheism is a philosophy of life that considers the welfare of humankind, rather than the interest of a supposed god or gods, to be of paramount importance. I maintain that there is no evidence of a supernatural power.

"Dr. North said, 'There are so many errors in the Bible that I don't really know where to start. I will mention one in particular, and if time permits, I could talk about many verses. But to start, Jesus tells his disciples in Matthew 16:28 (NKJV), "Assuredly, I say to you, there are some standing here who shall not taste death till they see the Son of Man coming in His kingdom." The people who were standing there all died, and they never saw Jesus return to establish a kingdom.'

"Dr. Eagle said, 'Along with being intolerant and pompous, Christians are very judgmental of other people who are not Christians. In discussions with others, their opinions are narrow-minded, based mainly on biblical dictates. They discuss many subjects and base their answers and comments on only what's in the Bible. They don't consider the opinion of others. And we know that the Bible has many errors and contradictions.'

"The Bible may be wanted by a few, but it is certainly not needed."

Mr. Cobra then said, "I will simply read two verses from wherever I open the Bible to. Let's see what it says." He flipped open the Bible. "I opened to **Ecclesiastes 4:1 (NKJV)**, and it says, 'Then I returned and considered all the oppression that is done under the sun: And look! The tears of the oppressed, But they have no comforter.' That doesn't sound very encouraging, does it? This book"—Mr. Cobra held the Bible in the air—"is certainly not a love letter." He turned and looked at the judge and said, "That's all I have, Your Honor."

Judge El-Bib pounded his gavel and instructed everyone to reconvene after lunch, at 2:00, for the closing statement of Mr. Devas.

CHAPTER 21

MR. DEVAS'S CLOSING STATEMENT

It was 2:00 p.m. The judge asked Mr. Devas to make his closing statement.

Mr. Devas walked to the area between the judge and the jury, and said, "Here is a quote from the Bible. ***Proverbs 18:17 (NKJV)***, *'The first one to plead his cause seems right, until his neighbor comes and examines him.'*

"Thank you and good morning, Your Honor and members of the jury. Mr. Cobra and his witnesses accuse the Bible of being ridiculous, stupid, cruel, vindictive, and many more extremes. However, the defense has presented a picture of **Jesus and the Bible as PERFECT LOVE**. I would like to take a few minutes to review some of the testimonies given to you by a few of the witnesses.

"There are several subjects that I would like to elaborate on. But first, the information that is on the monitor is very simple—just five words to help you remember the importance of the Bible in your life."

B	**Basic**
I	**Instructions**
B	**Before**
L	**Leaving**
E	**Earth**

IS THE BIBLE NECESSARY?

"That is really what the Bible is all about—**basic instructions before leaving earth**. In other words, the Bible is God's love letter to us, which includes the principles for living an abundant (joy-filled) life. The Bible contains the most fundamental and important information for you and all the world now and all future generations, before you join God.

"We realize that some of you may not be familiar with the Christian doctrines, principles established through past decisions. The primary ones are as follows: Believe that the Bible is true from cover to cover. Believe in God the Father. Believe in God the Son, who is Jesus Christ. Believe in God the Holy Spirit. Believe in Christ's death for all sins. Believe in His resurrection and ascension to heaven. Believe in Christ's second coming sometime in the future.

"And—" He paused. "I'd like to put forth a suggestion that you review, during your deliberations, what the Bible has to say about Christian doctrines. I don't want you to take my word for anything I have said, but you must investigate a few of the books in the Bible. I suggest that you start reading the books of Genesis, Proverbs, Psalms, Matthew, John, and Acts. If you ban future printing of the Bible, how will you or any of the world's seven billion people find the truth that lies within the pages of the Bible?

"I truly believe that you have received sufficient information and overwhelming evidence that Jesus, who is called the Christ, was a living, breathing human being and the Bible that Christianity says is the love letter from Jesus is faultless. Christianity's claims are substantiated by archaeology, science, and Bible translations. Archaeologists have verified the validity of many biblical details by the discovery of hundreds of artifacts and inscriptions and locations of many biblical cities. There is a lot of physical evidence for ancient history that is indicated in the Bible.

"We know that the Bible we have today is accurate, based on the Dead Sea Scrolls, the Codex Sinaiticus, the Codex Vaticanus, the Masoretic Text, and also the history of translations for thousands of years. As for science, there is a chart in your computers indicating that the Lord revealed many scientific facts in His Word thousands of years before man discovered them. These were submitted to you earlier by our witness, Dr. Lamb.

"So if the Bible itself is precise, *wouldn't* the messages about the events, people, and locations in the Bible be precise also? The Bible is the most reliable historical source where archaeological, scientific, and other historical records match secular writings outside of Scripture. *History tells us that man is not the source of our answers but the root of our problems. The Bible has the answers.*

"Evolutionists claim to know the origin of the universe. However, God explains the creation of the universe in the Bible, in the books of Genesis and John. The Bible, in the book of Genesis, tells us about creation. **Genesis 1:1 (NKJV)** says, 'In the beginning God created the heavens and the earth.' The Gospel of John also mentions the creation. In **John 1:1–3 (NKJV)**, it says, 'In the beginning was the Word, and the Word was with God, and the Word was God. He was in the beginning with God. All things were made through Him, and without Him nothing was made that was made.' The term *WORD* represents Jesus. God created everything on earth and the universe.

"Mr. Cobra's witnesses stated that the Bible has errors. But let me share with you four verses concerning Mary Magdalene, a follower of Jesus who went to the tomb of Jesus and witnessed the empty tomb. There are *differences in the four gospel accounts* but no errors in the Bible at all. The four authors, Matthew, Mark, Luke, and John, were witnesses, or they were writing for witnesses. If the event was described exactly the same, we would know that they copied from each other. But that is not the case! In each situation, Mary Magdalene saw an angel, as indicated in the four verses from the four gospels. This is the common fact expressed in each account.

"**Matthew 28:1–2 (NKJV)** says, 'Now after the Sabbath, as the first day of the week began to dawn, Mary Magdalene and the other Mary came to see the tomb. And behold, there was a great earthquake; for an angel of the Lord descended from heaven, and came and rolled back the stone from the door, and sat on it.'

"**Mark 16:1, 5 (NKJV)** says, 'Now when the Sabbath was past, Mary Magdalene, Mary the mother of James, and Salome bought spices, that they might come and anoint Him… And entering the tomb, they saw a young man clothed in a long white robe sitting on the right side; and they were alarmed.'

"**Luke 24:4, 10 (NKJV)** says, 'And it happened, as they were greatly perplexed about this, that behold, two men stood by them in shining garments… It was Mary Magdalene, Joanna, Mary the mother of James, and the other women with them, who told these things to the apostles.'

"**John 20:11–12 (NKJV)** says, 'But Mary stood outside by the tomb weeping, and as she wept she stooped down and looked into the tomb. And she saw two angels in white sitting, one at the head and the other at the feet, where the body of Jesus had lain.'

"Each witness's description of the event complements what the other witnesses saw—with no contradictions, only differences. Let's say there was a car accident with four witnesses. All four submit a different report of what they saw, but all four witnesses' accounts are clearly accurate.

"Many critics accuse the Bible of numerous errors until archaeological digs or another event proves that the scriptures are true. Unlike a citizen of the world who is charged with an offense and considered innocent until proven otherwise, the Bible is guilty until evidence shows it to be true. The Bible should be read with at least the same presumption of accuracy given to other literature that claim to be nonfiction.

"We have presented undeniable evidence that the Bible is flawless. The Bible must be presumed to be innocent of all charges and allowed to be printed and circulated. This is the way we approach all human communications. If we did not, life would not be possible. If we assumed that road signs and traffic signals were not telling the truth, we would probably be dead before we could prove otherwise. If we assumed food packages were mislabeled, we would have to open up all cans and packages before buying. Likewise, the Bible, like any other book, should be presumed to be telling us what the authors said, experienced, and heard. But negative critics begin with just the opposite presumption. Little wonder that they conclude that the Bible is riddled with error, whereas it is NOT!

"One of Mr. Cobra's witnesses said that we indoctrinate our children and teach with our own interpretation. But the Bible directs us to 'train up a child in the way he should go, And when he is old he will not depart from it' (**Proverbs 22:6 NKJV**). That is exactly what Christian teachers and parents strive to do.

"When children are born to us, we want them to follow God's direction for their own safety and happiness. Jesus has the same desire for us as His children. Since Jesus, God the Son, created us, should He not know what is best for us to live a good life? Jesus directs parents to discipline their children, but in a loving way. That is why He gave us a love letter, the Bible, to direct and guide us so that we may make the best choices for this life for us and our children. Should we not follow all His directions? Where are all His directions found?" Mr. Devas shrugged. "You have it." He pointed at the jury. "His directions are in His love letter, the Bible. So you see, the Bible truly is the most important book in the world for all time.

"How can one respond when accused of being biased (unfairly prejudiced for or against someone or something)? I know we all have our own ideas that we simply assume to be true but that may not be grounded in facts or proof. These foundational ideas are called presuppositions. A presupposition is something taken as being true or factual and used as a starting point for a course of action or reasoning. A couple of days ago, one of Mr. Cobra's witnesses described most Christians as being intolerant, unforgiving, arrogant, or pompous. Really? I would say some people in general may act this way once in a while, but most? No adult can claim to be completely neutral in most situations because our past experiences make up who we are and what we believe. If we have breath, we have bias! This affects how we think and how we interpret evidence. There is good evidence that Christian presuppositions are actually true. Some people have always questioned the accuracy of the Bible. For example, archaeologists and scientists have challenged many biblical details, only to later discover proof that the Bible's historical record is accurate."

Mr. Devas walked closer to the jury and said, "Self-help books abound on the web and in bookstores. They are not banned even though they may have conflicting solutions to life's problems. If the

IS THE BIBLE NECESSARY?

Bible, authored by the Creator, is the greatest and most reliable self-help book, shouldn't everyone be allowed and encouraged to read and study it? Or should we give in to unfounded fears and deny many people the lifesaving principles found in this, the ultimate self-help book? If so, tear up the Bible and throw it away."

Mr. Devas tore pages out of what looked like a Bible but was not, and he started to throw the pages out of the window. As he did so, a solid-white dove swooped down from a window ledge, grabbed a page of the Bible, and flew out another window.

"WOW! What just happened here?"

There was a deafening commotion as the people in the courtroom were startled and talked loudly over one another. Judge El-Bib pounded his gavel and demanded quiet. "If there are any more disturbances, I will clear the courtroom. Mr. Devas, no more theatrics!"

Mr. Devas responded, "Yes, Your Honor. As I mentioned earlier, Mr. Cobra and his witnesses accuse the Bible of being ridiculous, stupid, cruel, vindictive, and many more extremes. However, the defense has presented a picture that shows that *Jesus and the Bible ARE ETERNAL LOVE.*

"*The Bible is a spiritual book written by a Spiritual Being for all spiritual beings, and you are those people*!

"A true Christian? Yes, there are some who claim to be Christians, but their behaviors don't reflect the Bible's teaching. A true Christian does not display those negative, sinful behaviors.

"You have patiently listened to a wide variety of witnesses. You have heard a considerable amount of information for you to assimilate and discuss in detail as you deliberate." Looking at the jury, Mr. Devas said, "I'd like to remind you that it is the prosecution's high burden of proof that is required to persuade you that the Bible is guilty. In this case before you, the opposing attorney has NOT presented sufficient evidence to convict. I encourage you to announce to the court a verdict of—" He paused. "—not guilty, along with a declaration that the Bible is innocent of all the vulgar charges that the opposition has accused it of.

"Further, one of Mr. Cobra's witnesses stated that Christians use the Bible as a crutch. Nothing could be further from the truth. The Bible is the Christian's foundation that raises up every Christian."

There was a final verse from the Bible that Mr. Devas recited slowly. "**Second Chronicles 7:14 (NKJV)**, 'If My people who are called by My name will humble themselves, and pray and seek My face, and turn from their wicked ways, then I will hear from heaven, and will forgive their sin and heal their land.' This is a guarantee from the Lord. If we do what He asks, He will then give us what we need. And who better knows what we need than God?"

He walked over to the jury box, stood back about five feet, and stated, "It has been a pleasure to appear before you in this important case." He looked at the judge, nodded and said thank you, then returned to his chair.

The bailiff asked all to rise. Judge El-Bib banged his gavel lightly, thanked the jury, and then proclaimed, "The trial has ended." Those in the gallery were asked to please exit quietly.

Although all jurors had agreed to work that Saturday, the next day, some would be attending a religious service the day after, Sunday. Judge El-Bib ordered a UN security guard to accompany the jurors to their individual religious services. The jury and lawyers were requested to return to the courtroom promptly at 10:00 a.m. the next day, Saturday.

The UN guards escorted the jurors to their hotel rooms.

YOU, THE READER OF THIS BOOK, ARE THE THIRTEENTH JUROR. YOU HAVE COMPLETED READING THIS BOOK, SO YOU HAVE A VOTE. CONSIDER ALL THE EVIDENCE AND COMMENTS CAREFULLY. WHICH SIDE SPEAKS THE TRUTH? THE TRUTH IS ALL THAT MATTERS.

CHAPTER 22

THE JURY DELIBERATES

On Saturday morning, clear and sunny skies awaited the jurors as they enjoyed their breakfast before proceeding by the assigned bus to the courtroom by 10:00 a.m. Although there were no spectators in the gallery, the lawyers were seated in their chairs, waiting for Judge El-Bib to enter and remind the jurors of their responsibilities.

Judge El-Bib entered the courtroom and presented a few general instructions. Then he said, "I will again read the general oath for jurors. This is the oath you all agreed to at the beginning of the trial. You have already been sworn in, so there is no need for you to repeat this oath. 'I swear that I will fairly try the case before this court and that I will return a true and honest verdict according to the evidence and the instructions of this court under the punishment of the law.' Do any of you have an objection?"

There were no comments from the jury.

Judge El-Bib continued. "Very well then. You will now be escorted to the jury room to begin your deliberations. If a critical question arises, notify the bailiff, and he will inform me. I will be in my office during all your deliberations." The judge also insisted that the verdict must be unanimous.

Upon entering the jury room, the jurors took seats at random, with the jury alternates off to the side. The judge assigned a clerk to keep an accurate record of all that was said during deliberations and to assist the jury at the beginning of their deliberations. The record of the trial and jury deliberations were secret and would be placed in the courthouse safe until the end of ten years. Everyone had been provided with paper and pen to take notes during the deliberations.

Before deliberations began, the clerk informed everyone that snacks and coffee were available at the back of the room, as were name tags. A few minutes were taken for personal introductions and small talk to lighten the mood and for the jurors to get to know one another before selecting a jury foreman.

After an in-depth discussion and closed vote, a woman named Madeline was selected. She then positioned herself in the center chair so all would hear her. She commented, "So much substance was mentioned during the trial. Why don't we take one issue at a time and discuss for a few minutes and then go to another subject? Let's make a list of suggested topics. What should be the first?"

For starters, Bob suggested a discussion of the Bible in general. Ellen thought a discussion of the witnesses, including their honesty and reliability, should come next. The additional subjects added to the list included (1) *whether the Bible is too demanding*, (2) *whether God is loving*, (3) *whether Christians are hypocrites*, (4) *the verse "Let Us make man in Our image,"* (5) *proof through archaeology*, and (6) *errors and contradictions in the Bible*.

*****

After lunch and four more hours of deliberation, the jury completed the first day (Saturday). Some jurors chose to attend church on Sunday, while the rest stayed in their rooms.

On Monday, there was a general discussion of a number of pertinent subjects mentioned the day before, with more subjects added. The general discussion lasted two and a half days.

At midday of day three, the forewoman suggested that a secret ballot vote be taken. The vote was evenly split, so Madeline commented, "We have some work to do."

Being confined together for such extended periods caused some of the jury members to get a little testy with each other. At one point, the bailiff came into the room to settle things down during an intense interchange between three jurors that was getting out of hand, with cursing and threats. After the bailiff was called in two additional times to stop heated arguments, the judge called the jury to his chamber. Of course, that was a private conversation, but afterward, all appeared calm.

An additional two days passed, and another secret vote was taken. The jury had a verdict. It was Friday. Because of the tension concerning this case, the jury decided to draft a very carefully worded statement to the judge. The forewoman informed the bailiff that they were ready to go into court with a verdict but would also like to read a statement to the court. The bailiff forwarded this information to the judge.

The weather had had a cooling trend the last few days, but over the last few hours, clouds had rapidly developed. Then a steady rain covered the entire city of Jerusalem. The media announced worldwide that the jury had a verdict.

People who had been waiting for hours in the hallway of the courtroom entered the gallery. A small crowd of one hundred or so gathered outside the courthouse for the announcement, then they flowed into the courtyard area.

The bailiff gave the statement to the judge, who read it quietly before allowing it to be read to the court. He then directed the bailiff to bring the jury into the courtroom. The time was 12:00 noon on Friday. When the judge asked if the jury had come to a unanimous verdict, Madeline, the forewoman, declared that they had. She said, "You indicated that a short statement could be read before issuing a verdict. Is that acceptable?"

Judge El-Bib replied, "You may, but please make it brief."

The forewoman started to read the statement but then began to cough uncontrollably after speaking only four or five words, before collapsing in her chair.

CHAPTER 23

THE JURY'S DECISION

Judge El-Bib pounded the gavel sternly. He ordered the bailiff to clear the gallery and ordered the UN guards to escort the jury to the jury room. Someone called 911, and the judge hurried over to check on Madeline. EMTs stationed on the first floor of the courthouse reached the courtroom within three to four minutes, and an ambulance rushed to the courthouse. There was no time wasted getting the forewoman into the ambulance and rushed to the hospital.

Three hours went by, and the judge had heard nothing from the hospital. So he dismissed the jury for the day, with instructions for them to be back in court by 10:00 the next morning.

By the time the jury arrived on Saturday morning, the judge had talked with the doctors at the hospital and did not have good news. Madeline had had a stroke and sadly would not be able to continue her duties on the jury.

After Judge El-Bib met with the first alternate and asked him a few questions and was satisfied with his answers, he directed the alternate to join the other jurors in the deliberations. This alternate had previously been sworn in and had been observing the courtroom and jury proceedings from the beginning.

At 11:00 a.m. on Saturday, the jury, with its new member, began a review of what was discussed previously and voted for a new jury foreman. Since Harold had been nominated before, with no objections or other nominations, he was confirmed as the new foreman.

After he accepted, a short review of the trial testimonies followed, before a UN security guard excused the jury for the rest of the day, per the judge's orders. The jury would return to court on Monday morning at 10:00.

Jury deliberations begin again

On Monday morning, concerned about Madeline, the jury inquired about her condition. Before resuming deliberations, Judge El-Bib informed them that she would make a full recovery.

Additional deliberations lasted all morning, until another secret vote was taken at 2:00 p.m. The jury had a verdict.

The jury, with the new member, reviewed and approved the statement for the judge that was to be read to the court. Harold informed the bailiff that a verdict had been reached and that the jury was ready to return to court. The bailiff delivered the statement to the judge, who then read it.

The jury entered the courtroom to read their statement and give their verdict. The time was 3:00 p.m. As mentioned before, the tension concerning this case was extremely high. Hundreds of millions of people around the world were watching on TV, listening to the radio, or following on social media. They were all anxiously waiting to hear the verdict.

It had been raining hard all morning, but just now there was a loud crash and a lightning strike that lit up the whole courtroom. Then there was another, and then a third. The lightning seemed very close. Was this unusual weather by design or by chance? Was it to get everyone's attention before the grand finale, so to speak?

When the room settled down, Judge El-Bib asked the foreman in a soft but commanding voice if they had a unanimous verdict.

Harold, the new jury foreman, rose slowly from his chair, cleared his throat, and said in a loud, clear voice, "Your Honor, we have a verdict. But may I first read our statement to the court?"

The judge nodded.

"Your Honor, Mr. Cobra's witnesses mentioned a few details about the Bible that are certainly open to question and debate.

IS THE BIBLE NECESSARY?

However, Mr. Devas's witnesses have convinced us, the jury, that a great portion of what is in the Bible seems to be a letter from God."

The gallery started applauding loudly. Judge El-Bib pounded his gavel sternly and demanded quiet.

Harold continued. "Most of us on the jury are not Christian but have decided to at least study the Bible and investigate the life of Jesus Christ." He laid the statement down on the jury rail and slowly took a deep breath as anticipation grew. "*We, the jury, find the Bible not guilty of all charges, which include crimes of conspiracy, manipulation, trickery, connivance, and cover-up. But more importantly, we declare the Bible innocent of all charges, and in our opinion, it should not have been on trial for anything.*"

At the reading of the verdict, there were three very bright lightning flashes, followed by five minutes of rain. Then the weather miraculously cleared to sunny skies. Loud yells were heard from the gallery, some yea and some nay, but it was overwhelmingly positive for the Bible. Judge El-Bib called for order, but it was hopeless.

The judge then advised those in the gallery to stay seated, and he directed six specially chosen UN guards to escort the jury out of the courtroom. The jurors were taken to the courthouse basement, where an unmarked van was waiting for them. They were then driven to a hotel, a different one from where they had been staying. The location was known only by the UN guards, the judge, and the attorneys. Judge El-Bib was not taking any chances with the safety of the jurors.

After the trial, Diane and I (Fred) asked our attorney, Joshua Devas, to tell us a little more about himself. After a long pause, looking directly into our eyes, He said with a soft but commanding voice, "You know who **I AM**!"

About the Author

Al Provost, a licensed civil engineer, worked for the city of Los Angeles for thirty-six years, until retirement. After retirement, the Lord put in his heart the desire to obtain a California building contractor's license in order to help local churches, friends, and family with building projects. He was honored and humbled to use his contractor and engineering skills and experience to help local churches with their building projects, including two new missionary homes, a 5,000 sq. ft. church classroom and office building, church hall renovations, and other projects. He also built a few homes for friends during this time.

Throughout Al's life, Jesus has touched him in so many ways that it's hard to count. It was only as he matured in his faith that he has been able to acknowledge how Jesus's love and care have guided him toward Him alone and the abundant life He has to offer. Because of Him, Mr. Provost became an avid student of the Bible and was led by the Holy Spirit to write this story to assist others' understanding and appreciation of what God has done for the whole world through the Bible.

The author may be contacted at amprovost@juno.com.

CPSIA information can be obtained
at www.ICGtesting.com
Printed in the USA
BVHW091958130622
639651BV00017B/262